Shrink to Fit

Answers to Your Questions About Therapy

Dale A. Masi, D.S.W.
Robin Masi Kuettel

Health Communications, Inc.
Deerfield Beach, Florida

www.hci-online.com

Library of Congress Cataloging-in-Publication Data

Masi, Dale A.
    Shrink to fit: answers to your questions about therapy / Dale A.
Masi and Robin Masi Kuettel.
      p. cm.
    Includes bibliographical references and index.
    ISBN 1-55874-620-X (trade paper)
     1. Psychotherapy—Popular works. 2. Consumer education.
I. Kuettel, Robin Masi, date. II. Title.
RC480.515.M37 1998
616.89'14—dc21   98-38164
                                                 CIP

Publisher: Health Communications, Inc.
              3201 S.W. 15th Street
              Deerfield Beach, FL 33442-8190

Cover concept by Robin Masi Kuettel
Cover illustrations by Larissa Hise

For

Allen Cooper

and

Steve and Ben Kuettel

with love.

CONTENTS

ACKNOWLEDGMENTS

Special acknowledgment to Bonnie Engelhart, M.S.W., for her thoughtful comments and insight into the therapy process.

And to Chip Canty of Pilgrim New Media for the perfect title; Renée Masi, for her suggestions for the cover; Dale Kaplan, M.S.W., and Arthur Schwartz, Ph.D., for their clinical expertise; Andrea Peirce for her hard work in the editing process; Eric Masi, Ed.D., for his insightful comments throughout; and our editors, the publisher and staff at Health Communications Inc.

INTRODUCTION

"Who needs a shrink? Not me!" most of us say. "I'm not crazy. I can handle things just fine on my own." Throughout our daily lives we may think we are not *that* upset, *that* out of control or even *that* sick to warrant seeing a shrink. We may feel disturbed or unhappy, but not in an extreme enough situation to turn to outside help. But why live like that?

Or maybe you are thinking, *Great idea, but I can't afford it—therapy is only for Woody Allen types who live on Park Avenue or celebrities in Hollywood.* Not so! Therapy is available to *anyone* who may seek it—in one form or another. You just have to know where to look.

Granted, it's not easy to admit that you may need help. Picking up this book shows you are open to the idea that therapy may help you feel better. In return, you will find some of the very answers to help you reach more of your individual emotional potential.

However, as in any other profession, there are good and bad therapists. Failure to get the therapist and type of therapy that are right for you could result in your problems becoming worse. We both know from our own personal and professional experiences that bad therapy happens, and more often than you think. But it doesn't have to happen to you and that's why we wrote this book. *Shrink to Fit* will assist you in making the smartest choices possible in selecting the best and most financially viable path for you.

Therapy is not the only path to take when feeling lousy. It is always optimal to look to friends and family for emotional support. But therapy can be a helping hand when friends, family and costly alternatives have yielded few or no results. Therapy can be a welcome life raft in a sea of emotional turmoil.

Therapy has done wonders for many people. The lives of countless men, women and children have improved dramatically with therapy. It has brought many people a deeper understanding of and hope for their relationships, improved their work and school performance, even helped to shape major life choices—and cast an entirely different light onto their perception of the future. Therapy done well can open unknown worlds, introducing new ways of solving seemingly insurmountable problems and, in some cases, completely reshape a life.

However, therapy *can* be a confusing option when seeking help with emotional strife. There are many disciplines and types of practitioners available. How can you find the best one for you and be sure you are getting the help you are seeking? How can you keep from feeling dissatisfied or, worse, ripped off? How can you be sure your goals are being met—within your budget—and how will you know when you are ready to leave the therapeutic relationship? *Shrink to Fit* will help you answer these questions and more.

With the advent of managed care, your options for mental health care through your insurance benefit are more limited than ever before. Managed care stresses the value of shorter treatment and the use of medication over talk therapy, and often seeks second opinions in cases of a questionable diagnosis. The focus on short-term goal-oriented mental health care means you need to be more organized and focused to maximize your time in the therapist's chair.

Caution and common sense are prerequisites for making a successful journey into therapy, and out again in due time. This book will help to demystify that journey. Therapists today are often viewed with the same awe as the priests, medical doctors and lawyers of yesteryear. Many people hire them without researching their background or checking their references and are willing to take their advice at face value and accept their diagnoses without question. In fact, most people find their therapists through the Yellow Pages! The simple truth is, however, that neither the therapist nor the consumer can fully benefit from this arrangement. As the consumer, you must take more control of the therapeutic process in order to meet the goal that inspired the journey: feeling better and doing better.

Shrink to Fit will help you understand the basics of therapy and its different methods; the credentials and areas of expertise your potential therapist may have; how to select the best therapist for your needs; how to focus your emotional issues to work on what *you* feel you need; what happens in a typical session; how to evaluate the process along the way; and how to leave when you are ready. We will also present some options for you to help your loved ones in need, as well as adjuncts and alternatives to therapy. With the advent of managed care, paying for therapy has also become more complex. *Shrink to Fit* will present a range of possibilities that make therapy possible for anyone who may seek it out, on any budget.

Specifically designed *Shrink to Fit* tools, in the form of checklists, will help you take a proactive role in the process by assessing and prioritizing your needs, setting goals, designing an action plan, planning a budget, interviewing potential therapists, journal keeping, and checking your progress to ensure therapy is being provided in the best and most effective way possible.

This book is meant to work in two ways: for the consumer new to therapy who needs a helping hand and information to dispel some myths; and for the seasoned consumer of therapy anxious for some additional tools in order to ensure therapy is progressing at the best pace for his needs. It is designed to be accessed throughout the entire therapy experience or as a resource to be consulted as needed.

By picking up this book, you have already begun to do your part. Doing your homework and a bit of research, listening to your instincts when they tell you that something is amiss with the therapist you are seeing or the process being initiated—these are your responsibilities as a consumer. We hope that this book will help you to take these important steps. You deserve the help for which you are looking—the help that will enable you to get your needs met, live a rich and fulfilling life, and be happy.

Shrink to Fit is designed as a personal guide through the therapy process for you, the consumer eager for an inside look at therapy. It is an arm-around-the-shoulder guide to navigating your way through the multitude of alternatives available to you.

[*AUTHOR'S NOTE:* Throughout this book, you will find client testimonials from individuals who are or have been in therapy. All names and identifying information have been changed or removed.

We have attempted to equalize the use of the pronouns *he* and *she* throughout the book.]

1

DOING YOUR HOMEWORK
What Is Therapy?

The term *therapy* has sometimes been laden with inappropriate or inaccurate meanings by the media and nonclinical professionals. "Seeing a shrink" often carries unpleasant associations of instability and an inability to stand on one's own two feet. Friends, relatives or coworkers may well have their own positive or negative ideas about therapy and what it can do. Men, in particular, have often been schooled to "tough it out" and, sometimes, to repress important feelings. If you are a newcomer to therapy, this input may have a profound effect on your comfort level with this approach to problem solving; you may wonder if this is a good direction for you to pursue. However, just as you should seek consultation from a physician when experiencing physical pain, it is a sign of emotional *health* to seek therapy as a relief from emotional stress.

What has worked for others, of course, may not prove successful—or even appropriate—for you. One person may start therapy because he simply feels stuck in resolving a relationship problem, although he has no apparent illness. Another may suffer from a mental illness with identifiable symptoms and need medication. Sometimes the decision to enter therapy is not one's own. Relatives, supervisors at work, or even the courts may be the ones to recommend or order therapy. Given the myriad reasons for embarking on therapy, how can one begin to understand how it works?

> *NEW TO THERAPY: Never having been to counseling of any kind, I was very nervous about going for marriage counseling. However, since we've gone, our marriage has greatly improved and my anxieties about counseling have disappeared. I strongly believe that was a very good move on our part!*

For the purposes of this book, individual therapy, defined as a face-to-face interaction between you and a trained professional, will be the primary type presented. Ideally, it results in the individual acquiring a deeper understanding of a situation and the way one's behavior contributes to it. The therapeutic process will also point to ways that behavioral changes can be made to improve the situation. The trained clinician steers the process in a direction that helps ensure that this will occur.

> *A NEW APPROACH TO LIFE: Greg made me more aware of my choices in handling situations in my life. It was very enlightening. I was encouraged to make my life more manageable and satisfying to me. This new approach will take much thought and time, but he has certainly, with much concern and understanding, given me a better way to deal with matters. His help and guidance have been a blessing to me.*

Therapy is neither pure art nor science, but a combination of the two. The type of therapy used is considered the "science." The ability to engage you—the client—in a dialogue through careful listening and interpretation of your thoughts and feelings is considered the "art."

What You Bring to the Individual Therapy Process

The key components that you can contribute to your success in therapy are a clarity of purpose, the motivation to change and the ability to trust another person (the therapist). The therapist, in turn, will offer sharp listening and interpretation skills, and filter these through the type of therapy that she practices.

The success of therapy also hinges on your motivation level, desire and capacity to make some changes within yourself or in your behavior (or both). Obviously the individual who pays for therapy and takes the time for the process is showing some level of commitment. Growth in therapy can be painful, so continued determination to work through the therapy process can be difficult. Too often, people give up and drop out.

> *TEARFUL BUT GETTING BETTER: I basically needed someone to listen to me and let me cry. Each visit is getting better. I'm beginning to get to know the counselor better and allowing myself to be more open.*

The key to successful therapy is trust: the ability to share with another human being one's deepest fears and perceived flaws. Trust presents a huge obstacle to many. As with the motivation to change, it is a critical factor. Without it, the chances of resolving your conflicts are slim. Therapy should allow you to express your emotions in a safe environment where you won't feel criticized or made to feel guilty.

As you enter a therapeutic relationship, you should try to define, as clearly as possible and with the therapist's help, what you hope to accomplish. (See chapter 2 for help in focusing your needs.) Defining the "why" in "Why am I here?" is critical for two reasons. It not only enables you to better judge if therapy is being helpful to you as the process takes off, but it gives both you and the therapist a barometer for gauging when therapy has reached a successful end. (See chapter 3 on the implementation of an action plan to help you in this phase of the process.)

The value of this type of insight cannot be overemphasized, particularly in today's setting of managed care, where the emphasis is on short courses of treatment. The economics of managed care demand that the goal(s) of therapy be sharply focused. In fact, the question of how insurance companies will apply mental health benefits in the coming decades (and therefore attempt to define therapy) have many clients and practitioners expressing serious ethical concerns. Increasingly, the therapists' and clients' perspectives on how therapy is shaped are not considered. Several professional associations—including the American Psychiatric Association, the American Psychological Association and the National Association of Social Workers—have filed suit against the major managed behavioral care providers, charging restraint of trade and collusion in pricing. (See chapter 7 for further reading on managed care and its implications.)

What the Therapist Brings to the Therapy Process

As for the therapist, it is critical that she find a style that enables you to articulate your needs and goals, express any discomforts, and continue to develop and grow. The therapist helps expand the client's capacity for change. In establishing a safe and reliable environment to share intimate information, the therapist enhances the client's ability to trust another human being. The therapist's talent in helping the client develop a trusting relationship where it feels safe to discuss fears and vulnerabilities and to consider making some changes is what makes therapy work.

The therapist's art lies in her ability to foster change despite an often notable lack of clarity, motivation and capacity to trust on the part of the client. Superior diagnostic skills and knowledge of specific theoretical schools of practice are also important. She brings experience talking to individuals under stress and helping them to not get sidetracked from their goals. These intangible qualities lie at the root of why there are so many therapists and types of therapy available in any given community. A therapist can practice one or several theoretical methods, as is relevant to each client.

Under the best of circumstances, the change initiated by therapy will help you to gain some confidence and optimism about your life and, of course, to feel better. Because of the many different types of therapies and therapists you are likely to find in your community, you should get a sense of what is available to you before making a selection. (See chapter 5 for tips on making the right choice.)

> *GENTLY HELPED TO RAISE SELF-ESTEEM: I met with Cheryl the first day I called, and follow-up sessions were scheduled conveniently after work. Cheryl helped me see how to gain some control in an almost uncontrollable situation. She helped me to see my harsh assessment of myself and gave me suggestions on how to ease up. She is warm, easy to talk to and gentle in her wise guidance. I really appreciate her help!*

2

ON THE COUCH OR OFF?
Does Therapy Make Sense for You?

- Mary Ann is a thirty-two-year-old mother of two who, after her husband leaves in the morning, finds herself sitting at the kitchen table in tears. She has devoured everything in the refrigerator and has gained fifteen pounds in the last two months.
- Sam needs several drinks to get through the workday. He's finding it increasingly difficult to get himself to work each morning. He also drinks at night. This morning he woke up with no memory of how he made it home.
- When Sally and Peter talk to each other, it is only to criticize one another. They yell, they argue. Or they are silent and withdrawn. Their teenagers are starting to act up at school.
- Jennifer feels that she and her husband no longer communicate well. As her depression deepens, she attempts to patch up the gaps inside of her by shopping,

charging countless items she hardly needs. She is terrified her husband will find out how much money she has spent.

Looking at these lives from the outside, it may seem obvious that these people need help. In fact, they are far from being unique in that regard. According to the National Institute of Mental Health, every year one in ten Americans experiences some disability from a diagnosable mental illness.[1] Approximately 40 percent of Americans will sit in a psychotherapist's chair at some point in their lives.[2]

Contrary to some people's opinion, the fact that you think you may need therapy doesn't mean you are crazy. Many of life's stresses are managed without therapy. However, sometimes things pile up and can greatly affect our ability to function in work or school, in relationships and in society in general. Very often it's when this occurs that therapy can be most useful.

The _Shrink to Fit_ Tools

In this book there are several tools designed to help you assess your needs and evaluate your progress in therapy. These are informal instruments designed to be used as guides to help you clarify your journey. Use any or all of the tools as suggested and revisit them when particular phases of your therapy are in question.

The tools are designed to help you stay on track through a potentially bumpy but illuminating process. Do not think of them as ways to direct the entire therapy process. Obviously, you are placing yourself in the hands of an expert for a reason. Your needs may shift dramatically once you begin to discover more about yourself in therapy. Therapy will reveal many mysteries. Remaining flexible in therapy is critical, as seemingly unrelated issues will probably surface during the process. But by doing this initial and ongoing work, you will save yourself considerable time and money, and probably a good measure of fear and anxiety.

It is suggested that you begin a journal at this stage in the process. Try to write down thoughts and comments about your particular situation that come up during your reading of the book and when going through the checklists. Using this book interactively will help you gain control of your thoughts and organize yourself to begin the journey of feeling better with therapy. You will also be asked to write in your journal after each session in therapy. Start now!

How to Tell If Therapy Is What You Need

You are now going to go through a phase of assessing your needs. In this first step, take a snapshot of your life as it is right now. Freeze all the elements—your feelings, your behavior, your situation—and pick them up as if they were a composite image on a piece of paper. Conducting a thorough self-assessment can help you learn an enormous amount about whether you need therapy, and about what type may be optimal for you.

As you begin this process, you may want to take note of the four basic situations in which someone's emotional health can be adversely affected. Perhaps one or more apply to you.

- Accumulation of life's normal stressors
- Trauma
- Living with a loved one's problem
- Recurring issues

Accumulation of Life's Normal Stressors

Life offers up numerous stresses, or "stressors." Perhaps there is more occurring in your life than you realize. Has a family member or friend recently died? Have you moved? Had a child? Bought a house? Recently gotten married? Recently filed for divorce? Are you caring for an elderly relative? These are just a few of the "life stressors" that many of us will experience throughout our lives. But while we all experience a number of them, we differ in our capacity to cope. Some of us deal with these stressors with a solid practicality and clarity, while others are drawn under, especially if they occur simultaneously or in quick succession.

> *A GRIEVING HUSBAND: Back in November 1997, just a month after my wife passed away, I started sessions with Nancy N., Ph.D. She helped me understand and deal with the range of emotions I was experiencing: loneliness, anger, grief and remorse. We added another hour-a-month therapy session to help get me through the first year. My last session with her was yesterday. I now know that once again I can be that lovable old man that I used to be.*

Thomas Holmes and Richard Rahe, psychiatrists at the University of Washington Medical School, have developed a life-crisis scale (see table 1).[3] They define a "life crisis" as the accumulation of at least 150 points in the table, when experienced in a twelve-month period. The risk for physical and emotional problems is notably high during the twenty-four months following a life crisis. Determine your level of "normal life stress" by adding up points based on this chart. Consider your life as it is at this moment. Sometimes simply knowing that these stressors exist, but can be lessened with time, can greatly improve your outlook on life.

Table 1
The Social Readjustment Rating Scale

Life Event	Mean Value
1. Death of spouse	100
2. Divorce	73
3. Marital separation	65
4. Jail term	63
5. Death of close family member	63
6. Personal injury or illness	53
7. Marriage	50
8. Fired at work	47
9. Marital reconciliation	45
10. Retirement	45
11. Change in the health of family member	45
12. Pregnancy	40
13. Sex difficulties	39
14. Adjusting to a new family member	39
15. Business readjustment	39
16. Change in financial state	38
17. Death of a close friend	37
18. Change to different line of work	36
19. Change [increase] in number of arguments with spouse	35
20. Foreclosure of mortgage or loan	31

Life Event	Mean Value
21. Acquiring and maintaining a mortgage of $100,000 or more*	31
22. Change in responsibilities at work	29
23. Son or daughter leaving home	29
24. Trouble with in-laws	29
25. Outstanding personal achievement	28
26. Spouse begins or stops work	26
27. Begin or end school	26
28. Change in living conditions	25
29. Revision of personal habits [dieting, starting an exercise program]	24
30. Trouble with your boss	23
31. Change in work hours or conditions	20
32. Change in residence	20
33. Change in schools	20
34. Change in recreation [joining a sports team or class]	19
35. Change in church activities	19
36. Change in social activities [planning a wedding, attending more social events than usual]	18
37. Mortgage or loan less than $100,000*	17
38. Change in sleeping habits	16
39. Change in number of family get-togethers	15
40. Change in eating habits	15
41. Vacation	13
42. Christmas	12
43. Minor violations of the law	11

*Authors' change to reflect today's economy.

If you are experiencing one or several of these life stressors, do not underestimate the impact they can have on your conscious and unconscious emotional state. Their effects can often be minimized or even erased with the support of a carefully chosen family member, friend, trusted colleague, religious guide (priest, minister, rabbi) or mentor. Sometimes even just changing one's diet, quitting smoking, taking a vacation or beginning an exercise program can improve one's stress level immensely.

A STRUGGLING PARENT: I realize now that I was trying—but unsuccessfully—to cope with my son's suicide years ago. I had never fully dealt with the grief. With the counselor's help, I am working through it by voicing my feelings, with some positive results.

Support groups can be found to help grapple with many stressful situations, including single parenting, weight loss, smoking cessation, getting separated or divorced, and contending with grief and loss. Contacting a local family service agency, community mental health center, church, synagogue or mosque may help you find the type of group you need. If the stressor persists or the effects seem unbearable, however, individual therapy may be warranted.

> *A SINGLE MOM IN NEED: Bonnie S. was a life pre-*
> *server for me during a time in my life when I felt I*
> *was having an emotional and physical breakdown. I*
> *was feeling an immense stress that felt like a huge*
> *rock was crushing me. During my visits, Bonnie*
> *offered helpful ideas for coping with all the stress of*
> *post-divorce, work and financial worries. She helped*
> *me to feel that things would work out and offered con-*
> *structive tips for cutting back where I could. I feel*
> *greatly relieved, better able to handle stress and raise*
> *a daughter as a single mom. I am grateful for having*
> *such a wonderful person with whom I could talk and*
> *begin to get well.*

Trauma

Next is the tragic category of bad things that can happen to any of us just by walking through life. Have you just had your home or car broken into? Were you mugged while out shopping or sightseeing? Have you just suffered a rape or molestation? Have you been diagnosed with a chronic or life-threatening illness? Have you suffered a major automobile or household accident? Unfortunately, there is no way around it: If you've experienced a trauma, you *will* experience some type of reaction. If you think you are immune, be warned: Denial (ignoring or acting like the issue doesn't exist) may be plaguing you as well. If these situations are not handled properly, you may be feeling the subtle—or not so subtle— effects of such traumas for years to come. Too many people try to bear up under such situations rather than letting themselves experience such emotions as fear, guilt and anger.

Support groups, rape crisis centers and other types of

organizations can provide quality care for individuals who have suffered traumas. They are often excellent alternatives to individual therapy. But sometimes the stress or emotional wounds inflicted by the trauma are simply too profound to cope with in any other way than one-on-one therapy. You may not be comfortable dealing with trauma in a group situation and feel the need for more individualized attention, a fear of exposure or the desire to move at your own pace. These are all perfectly appropriate reasons for you not to want to join a support group; therefore, one-on-one therapy may be the answer for you.

> *STRUGGLING: I was dealing with depression as a result of being diagnosed with advanced ovarian cancer and was also contending with the physical problems associated with it. I had very little energy or will to fight the cancer. Counseling helped me deal with the problems in a more positive way. I no longer feel like I was dealt a death sentence. I am better able to manage my emotions and fears.*

Living with a Loved One's Problem

Are you living with or close to someone with an emotional problem? A mental disorder? Experts have only recently recognized the immense stress that the presence of such an individual can cause in a family. Katherine Graham, former editor of the *Washington Post*, describes this vividly in her book *Personal History*, when she describes what it was like living with her husband, Phil Graham, a bipolar manic depressive who committed suicide:

> *Phil's behavior grew more and more erratic. Things were getting very bad and much more public, but we all excused his angry, aberrant moods as signs of exhaustion. . . . He began to turn on everyone around him with incredible explosions of anger.*[4]

Another example of the effects of living with a mentally ill individual can be seen in Clea Simon's book *Madhouse: Growing Up in the Shadow of Mentally Ill Siblings.* She writes about her schizophrenic older sister, Katherine, whom she said wanted to play with her [Simon's] precious pet hamster. Katherine wanted to teach the hamster to play piano:

> *I tried to stop her from placing the little round animal on the keyboard. . . . but she ignored my protests and soon was chuckling, then roaring with laughter as his pink feet depressed the keys. . . . Powerless in the face of her single-minded zeal, I watched my golden-furred pet, wide-eyed and frantic, run his chromatic scales. Then, glancing up at her, I saw her manic grin turn vicious. I held my breath, waiting for the explosion, hoping that if I was quiet, maybe she wouldn't lash out. . . . Moments before she "accidentally" slammed the keyboard cover down, crushing my pet, I was ordering myself: Don't care. You can't do anything, so don't care. I was already retreating into my own safe inner space.*[5]

Is someone you love addicted to alcohol, drugs, gambling, or have an eating disorder or a sexual addiction? It is critical in such instances—regardless of the particular addiction—to shift your focus off the other person and onto yourself. Individuals living with addicts often adjust their lives to the moods and using patterns of the addicted person. Instead, you need to concentrate on your *own* needs and let go of your constant preoccupation with the addict. This may sound cruel or even impossible, but it will prove critical for you and your loved ones as you try to find a way to live happy and healthy lives. It is always more productive to change internally rather than try to get somebody else to change.

> *A SPOUSE GETTING BETTER: I saw Joyce because of marital problems caused by my husband's gambling, his work-related problems, his unhealthy relationship with his abusive father and his sibling's attempt at suicide. As his wife, I am placed in a difficult position more often than not. Joyce helped me reaffirm my strength and to take better care of myself.*

It has been found that for every alcoholic in a family, approximately four other family members are affected and may need outside help to cope. Alternatives to therapy for those living with a loved one's problems include such groups as Al-Anon, NARACOM and support groups for the families of the mentally ill. You may want to pursue them along with therapy, which may speed up and ensure complete recovery. Some benefits of joining a support group or Twelve-Step program are that they can deepen your understanding of the addiction or mental illness, and its participants can offer practical tips and other resources related to living with that particular affliction.

Living with and trying to control somebody struggling with an addiction or mental illness can have a serious and often debilitating impact. If you are seeing a therapist, he can help you understand what is happening to you and your loved one as you try to cope with this dynamic.

Recurring Issues

Do you frequently find yourself in abusive, dead-end relationships? Do you feel that boss after boss in job after job takes advantage of you? Are you unhappy with things in general, but are unable to identify why? Chances are you have ongoing issues that are causing you to repeat certain self-destructive behavior. This is frequently seen in cases where persons will divorce an alcoholic spouse and proceed to marry another alcoholic. This is one of the most difficult characteristics to assess and resolve because it may involve breaking through years of denial about yourself and your behavior.

If any of the following apply to you, they may signal ongoing emotional difficulties that are hampering your daily life:

- Somebody (an employer, doctor, friend, relative, spouse, child, the courts) has suggested you seek counseling.
- You are thinking of making a major life change, be it in a relationship, career choice, religious affiliation, sexual orientation or place that you live. Does this make sense for where you are right now, or are you really escaping other issues? For example, substance abusers are known for moving their residences, thinking that the next place they land will somehow be better and they will not drink or use.
- Your emotional pain has become more than you can handle. You may develop symptoms of stress: insomnia, nightmares, intense anxiety or even panic attacks. You

may find you have a short temper, go on spending sprees, drink more than usual or overeat.

> *A THANKFUL SURVIVOR: Amy helped me immensely. I came to her at a time when there was no peace in any part of my life. My son was a serious drug addict, I was in jeopardy of losing my job and my marriage had disintegrated. Amy has helped me gain back my self-esteem, not be paralyzed by the thought of layoffs, wean myself from my codependent relationship with my son and open my eyes to a very emotionally abusive marriage that I decided was best to end. I literally owe her my life!*

Warning Signs Checklist for Considering Therapy

This is the first in a series of *Shrink to Fit* tools to help guide you through the process of beginning therapy. This checklist can be used as a barometer of your emotional health. The items are presented as "triggers" for you to consider what is happening in your life today. Or they may bring up issues for you not mentioned here. As you review the list, ask yourself whether any apply to you. Try to be as honest and straightforward with yourself as possible.

Check off those that apply and write comments in your journal to expand your thoughts. Rate your response on a point scale of: mild = 1–2, moderate = 3–4, severe = 5–6. It is important to note that many small, or mild, items can affect you as much as one severe one. Often we wait too long to get help—

until problems snowball into a crisis. Write in your journal for as long as necessary when going over this checklist. Repeat the list a few times and be sure you've exhausted every possibility.

Family History

- ☐ Does your family (parents or siblings) have a history of domestic violence?
- ☐ Does your family have a history of sexual abuse?
- ☐ Does your family have a history of alcohol or drug abuse?
- ☐ Does your family have a history of gambling?
- ☐ Does your family have a history of shoplifting?
- ☐ Does your family have a history of overeating or eating disorders?
- ☐ Does your family have a history of philandering or extra-marital affairs?
- ☐ Were there any major fluctuations in your family's income—either bankruptcy or instant wealth?
- ☐ Were you strictly disciplined either verbally or physically?
- ☐ Did you move frequently as a youngster? (More than eight times in eighteen years?)
- ☐ Do you have very little memory of your childhood?
- ☐ Were you raised with very strict religious practices?
- ☐ Do you feel there were any unusual circumstances surrounding the death(s) of your pet(s)?
- ☐ Does anyone in your family have a history of, or has anyone in your family been hospitalized for, mental illness?
- ☐ Has anyone in your family committed suicide?
- ☐ Did either of your parents die, or were they severely disabled, when you were young?
- ☐ Do you consider your family extremely dysfunctional?

☐ Are there certain close family members with whom you do not speak?

☐ Did you experience any catastrophic events that greatly impacted your childhood (e.g., flood, fire, homelessness)?

☐ Do you feel that you have been abandoned by your family?

Relationship

☐ Do you have trouble being intimate with others?

☐ Do you have a serious problem with commitment?

☐ Have you been told you have a problem with getting close to another person or making a commitment?

☐ Do you avoid honest, face-to-face conversations with your spouse/partner?

☐ Do you have trouble making or keeping friendships?

☐ Are you unable to apologize or take responsibility for wrongs you know you have done?

☐ Are arguments with your spouse or partner getting more frequent and explosive?

☐ Do you always place the blame for your failing relationship on your partner?

☐ Do you feel shame about your past behaviors in relationships?

☐ Are you having any serious marital or intimate relationship difficulties?

☐ Do you no longer wish to be married and yearn for the single life?

☐ Have you or your spouse/partner engaged in an extramarital affair(s)?

☐ Are you or your spouse considering a divorce?

☐ Are you in the process of separating from or divorcing your spouse/partner?

- [ ] Do you continually seek contact with or try to help or change people who cause you great pain?
- [ ] Do you think you can make people change their destructive behaviors?
- [ ] Are you surrounding yourself with people who do not treat you well or care about you?
- [ ] Do you feel you only exist to take care of others?
- [ ] Are you loyal to someone who has betrayed you?
- [ ] Do you have trouble setting limits on your time, money or anything else?
- [ ] Do you isolate yourself from friends and family, avoiding opportunities to spend time with them?
- [ ] Are you spending more time at work or traveling to avoid your home life?
- [ ] Do you volunteer (in the community or elsewhere) primarily to get out of the house?
- [ ] Are you spending excessive time in front of the TV set or at the computer to avoid your primary relationships?
- [ ] Are you having problems with your children?
- [ ] Are you having trouble being the parent you want to be to your children?
- [ ] Has your child been recently diagnosed with a serious developmental, physical or emotional disorder?
- [ ] Have you given up a child for adoption or had an abortion and still live with unresolved feelings?

Physical

- [ ] Do you seem accident prone?
- [ ] Do you have sleeping problems?
- [ ] Are you overeating, or have you lost your appetite?

☐ Have you dropped or gained weight unintentionally?

☐ Are you having serious trouble concentrating?

☐ Do you feel a notable lack of energy (e.g., can't get out of bed, taking extended naps)?

☐ Have you lost interest in activities that you used to look forward to?

☐ Are you crying more than usual, in public places or before other people, causing yourself embarrassment?

☐ Are you experiencing an unusual number of headaches? Have they increased in severity?

☐ Have your asthma attacks or allergies increased?

☐ Are your migraines under control, or are they interfering with your life? Have they increased lately?

☐ Do you have excessive hives or unexplained rashes?

☐ Are you having trouble conceiving a child?

☐ Are you starving yourself or binging on food and then purging (taking laxatives or forcing yourself to vomit)?

☐ Do you keep going to a doctor because you are convinced that something is wrong, but have never gotten a solid diagnosis?

☐ Has somebody close to you expressed concern at your deteriorating appearance?

☐ Have you had a series of minor accidents or illnesses?

☐ Has someone you are close to been seriously ill or in a serious accident?

☐ Are you caring for an ill or aging relative?

☐ Are you having difficulty with the physical changes of menopause, menstruation or pregnancy?

☐ Are you having difficulty with a disability or chronic pain?

☐ Are you extremely conscious of bodily changes due to the aging process?

Job/School

- [ ] Has your performance at work or school deteriorated?
- [ ] Do you find yourself going in late for no valid reason, or taking sick or vacation days when not necessary?
- [ ] Do you hop from job to job with no apparent reason?
- [ ] Do you have difficulty getting along with your boss or coworkers?
- [ ] Are you afraid of a coworker?
- [ ] Are you being sexually harassed?
- [ ] Do you dislike your job?
- [ ] Do you take risks sexually at work?
- [ ] Do you have difficulty meeting important deadlines?
- [ ] Has your supervisor or teacher warned that your work is unacceptable?
- [ ] Have you recently been suspended or fired?
- [ ] Are you the target of unwarranted anger from others at work?

Self-Awareness

- [ ] Do you find yourself taking more diet pills, sleep aids, anti-depressants, illegal drugs, or any other over-the-counter or prescription medicine?
- [ ] Do you always need some type of medication (over-the-counter, prescription, alcohol) to get to sleep?
- [ ] Has someone spoken to you about your self-medication practices?
- [ ] Do you feel you have lost your sense of humor?
- [ ] Do you have trouble with change? Does it stop you from doing the things you'd like to be doing?
- [ ] Do you feel you are overly responsible for others?

☐ Has your thinking become stuck in "black or white," with no room for external input or variations in thought patterns?

☐ Have your religious practices become excessive in time, money or attention?

Sexual Activity

☐ Are you pregnant and do not want to be?

☐ Have you lost interest in sex, or do you find yourself unable to perform sexually?

☐ Do you feel sexually "turned off"?

☐ Are you sexually promiscuous in ways that are unusual for you?

☐ Are you involved in sexual practices (unprotected sex, sadomasochism, prostitution) that make you fearful, ashamed or uncomfortable?

☐ Do you think you may have a sexual addiction?

☐ Are you having or considering an extramarital affair?

☐ Are extramarital affairs a frequent occurrence in your life?

☐ Do you feel the need to fantasize to get away from being in the present during sex? Is it getting in the way of being intimate with your partner?

☐ Is your primary sexual relationship via the Internet or the telephone (e.g., engaging in telephone sex, visiting Web sites and/or chat rooms with sexual content)?

☐ Are you engaging in sexual activity with prostitutes?

☐ Are you using pornography in a way that does not feel normal to you?

☐ Are you worried about your partner's use of pornography?

☐ Are you worried about your partner's sexual practices?

Addictions/Substance Abuse

☐ Has your use of a particular addictive substance—alcohol, marijuana, cigarettes, illegal drugs—increased lately?

☐ Do you find yourself worrying about your use of any particular substance?

☐ Are you worried about your gambling?

☐ Do you drive while under the influence of drugs or alcohol?

☐ Have you experienced blackouts?

☐ Has somebody spoken with you about your alcohol, drug use or gambling?

☐ Is someone you are close to addicted to alcohol, drugs or gambling?

☐ Do you suspect someone close to you of having an eating disorder?

☐ Do you suspect someone close to you of having a sexual addiction?

Financial

☐ Do you find yourself spending money that you do not have?

☐ Have you "maxed out" your credit cards?

☐ Do your financial worries keep you from sleeping?

☐ Are you spending money you don't have on the lottery?

☐ Are you unable to speak to your primary partner about financial issues?

☐ Are checks bouncing?

☐ Are collectors calling?

☐ Is your business about to go bankrupt?

☐ Have you declared personal bankruptcy?

☐ Are you considering illegal methods (stealing, embezzling, cheating on taxes) to pay off mounting debts?

Trouble with the Law

☐ Have you been caught or arrested for shoplifting, reckless driving, domestic violence, or driving while under the influence of alcohol or drugs?

☐ Do you feel the police are keeping an eye on you?

☐ Has someone filed a restraining order against you?

☐ Have you violated parole or probation?

☐ Have you committed a misdemeanor or felony?

Depression

☐ Do you sometimes feel physically drained and unable to move?

☐ Are you sleeping an unusual amount or, on the other hand, having trouble sleeping?

☐ Do you frequently wake up at night or early in the morning for no apparent reason?

☐ Are you experiencing recurring nightmares or hallucinations?

☐ Do you feel unloved, unwanted or lonely most of the time?

☐ Are you becoming uncharacteristically sloppy in your appearance?

☐ Has life lost much of its meaning for you?

☐ Do you care little about living?

☐ Have you said to someone close, "I'm afraid I'm depressed"?

Anxiety

☐ Are you having obsessive thoughts about someone or something?

☐ Have your personal habits become increasingly compulsive or repetitive?

☐ Has someone spoken to you about your obsessive or compulsive habits (e.g., constant hand washing, bathing or cleaning, or repeatedly checking safety items such as locks or smoke alarms)?

☐ Are you hoarding or collecting things excessively? Are there rooms in your home that you can no longer walk into?

☐ Do you sometimes have trouble breathing for no physical reason?

☐ Have you experienced a panic attack?

☐ Are you unable to do certain things because of your fears?

☐ Are you unable to engage socially because of your fears?

Suicide

☐ Are you having suicidal thoughts?

☐ Have you ever attempted suicide?

Violence

☐ Have you recently abused—either verbally, physically or sexually—your spouse/partner, child or anyone else?

☐ Has your emotional fuse gotten shorter?

☐ Are you frequently losing your temper?

☐ Do you find yourself driving very aggressively?

☐ Do you feel God is telling you to do things that make you feel uncomfortable?

☐ Do you get into scuffles with coworkers or strangers?

☐ Are you afraid of your anger toward your children or spouse/partner?

☐ Are you worried about somebody else's potential violence toward you or your children?

☐ Is someone monitoring your behavior, making you fear a

violent response (i.e., if you do not behave a certain way, you may experience violent consequences)?

If you review your checklist and have a number of "mild" or "moderate" answers (more than eight), or even just a few "severe" ratings, you may need to consider seeking help in therapy.

If you find a number of these warning signs in yourself, take a deep breath. Fight off rationalizations that may cloud your thinking. You might think, *Everybody has problems* or *I can handle it*. You may see some of the above warning signs but manage to convince yourself that you are doing fine on your own. Or you may be thinking, *Okay, I bought the book, but my problems are not so bad; they must be talking about more extreme situations*. This is a tough step to get through. If you feel ambivalence, fear or apprehension at this stage, consider it normal. No one likes to think that she needs outside professional help. Remember, it is a sign of health to be able to ask for help.

> *USED TO BE AFRAID OF THERAPY: I never thought I could nor would use a counselor. I am surprised and pleased, and no longer afraid to see a therapist. It was incredibly helpful to talk to a non–family member, non–coworker. I hope I won't have to use the service again but am glad to know they are there. John, my therapist, was great! His calm demeanor and concern made me so much less fearful of talking openly.*

By conducting your own personal self-assessment, you can begin to draw up a concrete plan of action.

Perhaps you simply need to:

- Seek out a trusted friend or family member
- Consult with your local minister, priest or rabbi
- Find a relevant support group

However, if more complex issues are present, it may make sense to pursue therapy.

Critical Signs Checklist for When to Enter Therapy

Sometimes there are feelings, thoughts and situations happening in our lives that must be addressed. They are usually very difficult to face and can be painful to manage on our own. This next checklist includes very real things many people experience in their lives.

If any of the critical signs are happening in your life, it is strongly recommended that you seek some type of therapy or outside help. These problems are very serious and will *not* dissolve on their own. There are many people who experience one or even several of these situations. There is help to deal with *all* of them. If *any* of these are occurring in your life, do not wait to get help. You only need to reach out and realize you are not alone.

Check any that are relevant and write comments in your journal.

☐ My psychological pain is preventing me from being the person I want to be.

☐ I have a secret or secret fear that I have never shared with anyone, and it is getting in the way of my life.

☐ I feel enormous shame about _____ (my sexual orientation, size, physical appearance, life circumstances, race, etc.).

☐ My physical pain is disturbing my life patterns, and I am not getting any relief.

☐ I am pregnant, do not want to be and have nowhere to turn.

☐ I have been raped or molested, and still feel the intensity of the feelings today.

☐ I was sexually abused as a child, and still feel the intensity of the feelings today.

☐ I suspect my spouse/partner or someone else is continually verbally abusing my children.

☐ I suspect my spouse/partner or someone else is physically abusing my children.

☐ I suspect my spouse/partner or someone else is sexually abusing my children.

☐ My spouse/partner or someone else is continually verbally abusing me.

☐ My spouse/partner or someone else is physically abusing me.

☐ My spouse/partner or someone else is sexually abusing me.

☐ I have just been physically or sexually threatened and do not know where to turn.

☐ I have just experienced my first incident of domestic violence and cannot tell anyone.

☐ I am very concerned about my alcohol/drug use or gambling.

☐ I am using illegal drugs and taking risks regarding my family or job (e.g., dealing at home or work, lying to partner or boss, appearing drunk or using on the job).

☐ My spouse/partner, boss, or friend has spoken to me about my alcohol/drug use or gambling.

☐ I am embezzling funds from work.

☐ I have stolen money or property to pay off debts.

☐ I have recently lost a loved one and do not know where to turn.

☐ I have just lost a child and cannot cope.

☐ I have been diagnosed with a chronic illness and feel overwhelmed.

☐ I have been diagnosed with a terminal illness and cannot cope.

☐ I have just been raped and cannot tell anyone.

☐ I have just had a serious auto accident and feel disoriented.

☐ I have just had a serious (other than auto) accident and feel unable to cope.

☐ I have just been arrested and feel overwhelmed.

☐ I intentionally cut myself to relieve my pain and desperation.

☐ I hit myself, and it makes me feel better.

☐ I am engaging in unsafe sex with prostitutes, call girls/boys or "escorts."

☐ I have frequent suicidal thoughts.

☐ I have a plan for committing suicide.

☐ I have fears that get in the way of living normally: of animals, elevators, heights, going outside, riding in a car or traveling in an airplane, for example.

☐ I have unintentionally gained more than 5 percent of my body weight in one month.

☐ I have unintentionally lost more than 5 percent of my body weight in one month.

☐ I am obsessed with one particular individual.

☐ I am stalking someone.

☐ I continually verbally abuse a family member, friend or someone else.

☐ I have physically abused a family member, friend or someone else.

☐ I am considering doing physical harm to someone.

☐ I have just gotten into a serious physical fight.

☐ I am worried about my potential for using a particular weapon (e.g., gun, knife).

☐ I am carrying a weapon (e.g., gun, knife) wherever I go and am seriously considering using it against one particular individual.

☐ I have sexually abused a family member, friend or someone else.

☐ I am having sexual fantasies about my children or somebody else's children.

The ability to recognize destructive things happening or that you are causing in your life is a major step in moving forward and feeling better. To admit to yourself that certain issues are happening in your life is a very courageous step.

Making Your Decision

Now *you* have to be the one to decide what your next move—if any—will be. If you have been honest with this self-appraisal, you may well have a surprise in store: You now have a sense of the behavioral issues complicating your life. Being armed with this knowledge *before* entering therapy will help give you control of the process and could help you recover more quickly.

A final recommendation: If you think you need help, start looking for it now. If you do not find the perfect person immediately, just begin. The most important thing is to start talking with *someone* about your problems. Talking to a physician, minister, priest, rabbi or teacher may help you clear up and crystallize your thoughts. While some physicians and religious practitioners are not well schooled in the particulars of therapy, they often can offer wise counsel. As for family members and friends, only confide in those whom you feel are wise and capable of being at least somewhat objective. Often the people who are closest to us are not necessarily our best resources. They may downplay the importance or seriousness of a situation, particularly if they have some connection to it. Tread carefully and choose wisely those individuals to whom you talk.

> *NO HELP FROM FRIENDS OR FAMILY: Family and friends were too free to tell me what they would do if they were in the same predicament. Their opinions actually angered me, and I pulled away from them. I needed to express myself and the way I felt with an understanding listener who didn't criticize everything that I did or did not do. I feel as if I have finally found the person I can relate to.*

Admitting there is a problem is the first—and often the hardest—step toward emotional health. Congratulations on completing this challenging task!

> *A DUTIFUL DAUGHTER: I cared for my mother for eight years, around the clock. She suffered from multiple strokes and Alzheimer's. When she died, it completely floored me. I couldn't shake the guilt and anger. I seemed not to care anymore about anything. The therapy I received made the difference. I'm much more myself again.*

3

CHARTING YOUR COURSE
Developing Your Action Plan and Knowing Your Rights

By taking control of your therapy before even starting to see a therapist, you can gain more confidence in your instincts, learn to trust yourself and gain a powerful sense of independence. By focusing your thoughts and emotions and being organized, you will help ensure that therapy will work for you.

Before seeing a therapist, you may find it helpful to develop an action plan. This is a blueprint of your goals, designed by you to delineate what *you* feel you need. By going through this exercise, you may find that although you don't feel in control of your life at this point, you can feel in control of your part of the therapy process.

Defining Your Goals

The last thing you may want to think through now are your goals. Most likely, you are focused on what you *don't* want more of (fighting, overspending, depression) and are hoping that what you *do* want more of in your life will simply develop from there. Start to consider what prompted you to consider therapy in the first place. Your goals may become more finely tuned as you undergo therapy.

Checking the Signs

Refer back to the warning signs and critical signs check-lists in chapter 2. Notice the items you checked and any others you may have added. See if most of your answers appear in a particular category. Add up the number of checkmarks from each of the thirteen sections of the warning signs checklist (family history, relationship, physical, job/school, self-awareness, sexual activity, addictions/substance abuse, financial, trouble with the law, depression, anxiety, suicide, violence) and note the sum next to each category. The categories with the highest numbers should indicate your primary area(s) of need. If no particular category stands out, examine which issues *within* the categories have been emphasized. Try to discern any particular trends.

Setting Goals

What would you like the *end result* of therapy to be for you? If you can define it here, great. If not, trust that it will surface during the process. Evaluating how your life can be *better* is in itself a healthy and cleansing exercise.

Perhaps your goal is to change jobs. Or maybe to develop a better relationship with your children, stop using drugs or alcohol, put a halt to self-destructive behavior, reconcile yourself to the loss of a loved one, take control of your finances, or file for divorce. Perhaps you are not even plagued by one particular problem, but want instead to begin an in-depth journey of self-discovery. Regardless of the goals, try to come up with concrete examples rather than vague wishes such as feeling happier, becoming more fulfilled or being nicer to others. If you are struggling with numerous issues, you should begin with the most urgent one.

Setting Your Boundaries

How much time and money can you give to the therapy process? Take stock of your finances, the time you have in your schedule (including time outside the office to reflect on the therapy experience) and your level of commitment to seeing the therapy process through. Develop a budget for the next six months (see chapter 7 for more on the financial aspects of therapy) and determine how much you can allocate to therapy. Look at your schedule: When is the best time for an appointment? During the day? Evenings? Weekends? Is child care an obstacle? How much distance are you willing to travel to the therapist's office?

Along with the time you actually spend meeting with the therapist, she may recommend that you take time to do some reading, writing in a journal, working on other assignments or attending a support group. The more you think through the extent of your commitment to these time issues *before* starting therapy, the better off—and less surprised or even resentful—you ultimately will be.

Certain minimums of money and time are usually necessary for staying focused and moving toward your goals. Can you commit to all of the following over a six-month period?

- A minimum of two to four full-session payments at $40 to $120, or two to four health insurance copayments at $10 to $50 each (for alternative payment options, see chapter 7)
- Two to four one-hour sessions per month
- Three to five hours a month devoted to development outside the therapist's office

If this type of commitment seems unrealistic to you, it may not be the best time to initiate therapy. However, beware of an important caveat: Make sure you are not rationalizing your way out of therapy. If you are in crisis, the time to make some serious sacrifices to get the help you need is now.

Accommodating Your Style

Some therapists use talk therapy only, others combine talk with role-playing, physical touch and physical performance. You should feel safe and comfortable in therapy, so it helps when the type of therapy you pick matches your style of thought and expression. Pose the following questions to yourself as you try to get a sense of the style that makes you most comfortable:

- Do you like to express your emotions verbally?
- Are you comfortable determining the topics you wish to discuss, or do you want the therapist to take the initiative?
- Do you tend to intellectualize your thoughts?
- Are you willing to role-play with your therapist or physically act out situations to unlock repressed emotions?
- Are you open to physical performance (punching a bag,

yelling, crying, dancing) or to subconscious exploration such as dream interpretation?

- Are you willing to be hypnotized?
- Are you willing to be touched by a therapist if a technique requires it?

Keep your answers to these questions in mind as you search for and interview a therapist.

AN OPEN-MINDED CLIENT: My experience with Sam was very helpful. It wasn't just talk. Doing mind exercises to recall issues in my past in order to change my subconscious made a big difference in understanding how I cope today.

Integrating Family Members into Therapy

Look at the relationship categories in your warning signs checklist. Is there a particular relationship that keeps coming up? You may want to bring in family members for additional work. (See chapter 11 for more information about family members in therapy.)

AN AGGRAVATED CLIENT: My wife joined us at the second session but could not continue. At the end of the session, she realized she needed help, too. We agreed that she should call our counselor, Shirley. Shirley was less than helpful and refused to see her. Now I cannot get my wife to call for another counselor. My wife and I are worse off than before we started counseling.

Some therapists believe that the first client or configuration (couple or family) they see is the primary client or therapeutic relationship. Therefore, if an individual from the couple or family wants to see the therapist on a one-to-one basis, the therapist may decline. Ideally, in this case, the therapist would refer you to another therapist or, at the very least, provide you with an answer that makes sense to you as to why she can't see you alone. Other therapists take a systemic point of view and feel they can work with each individual and unit simultaneously.

> *A SATISFIED CLIENT: Karen was well informed about areas we could explore and recommended some additional reading that was helpful as well. She worked very well with my husband and me jointly and in individual sessions. Karen was very helpful in coaching us to understand our relationship issues and focus on actions we could take.*

Creating Your Action Plan

Using the items you checked off on the two checklists in chapter 2 and considering the questions raised earlier in this chapter, complete your action plan. The half hour or so you take to develop this action plan could save you valuable time in therapy. Write down your responses to each item in your journal or in the space provided. Feel free to write as much as you can.

1. I am considering seeking therapy because:

   _____

   _____

2. My primary area of need is [*circle one from the warning signs checklist in chapter 2*]: family history, relationship, physical, job/school, self-awareness, sexual activity, addictions/ substance abuse, financial, trouble with the law, depression, anxiety, suicide, violence. If you checked off any of the items on the critical signs checklist, include them here. Explain to yourself on paper why this is a particular area of need. Be specific.

   _____

   _____

3. My secondary area of need is [*circle one*]: family history, relationship, physical, job/school, self-awareness, sexual activity, addictions/substance abuse, financial, trouble with the law, depression, anxiety, suicide, violence. Explain to yourself on paper why this is a particular area of need. Be specific.

   _____

   _____

4. My goals in therapy are:

   a. _____

   b. _____

   c. _____

   Comments: _____

   _____

5. I can allocate $_____ [*amount*] per month.

6. I can allocate _____ [*number*] one-hour sessions per month.

7. I can allocate _____ [*number*] outside hours per month.

8. I am willing to commit _____ [*number*] months to this process.

9. I prefer verbal/nonverbal communication [*circle one*].

10. It may be useful to work with _____ [*family member/significant other*] at some point during the process.

I, _____ [*your signature*], commit to the above for a six-month period. (*This is only a commitment to yourself and is not necessarily for your therapist to see.*)

Check back with your action plan if, weeks or months from now, you start to feel off-track or dissatisfied with therapy, or are even considering leaving.

Congratulations! By committing to this action plan, you have taken another important step to ensure that therapy will be a satisfying and successful experience.

AN ACTION PLAN SUCCESS STORY: The action plan the counselor and I developed during our session was very useful, and I think it not only improved the current situation, but was also useful in many other areas of my life. Stressing the importance of "small successes" was very important and useful to me.

Client Rights

Patients should be able to get more information to help them choose their doctor, including how much experience they have, whether they have been disciplined and whether they get financial incentives from health plans to withhold care.

—FROM THE REPORT OF PRESIDENT CLINTON'S ADVISORY COMMISSION ON CONSUMER PROTECTION AND QUALITY IN THE HEALTH CARE INDUSTRY, NOVEMBER 20, 1997

You are about to tell a complete stranger incredibly personal things about your life. How can you be sure that she can be trusted and will keep what you say in confidence? As a client, you have certain rights. Know them.

The Presidential Advisory Commission on Consumer Protection and Quality in the Health Care Industry, formed in 1997, has drawn up a "patient's bill of rights." This includes subjects such as information disclosure, patient choices, appeal procedures, participation in treatment decisions, handling of emergencies and confidentiality of records. It is clearly recognized today that clients/patients have rights. Along with this comes your responsibility to be informed. Therapists are aware of these rights, so do not feel intimidated when exercising them.

The Code of Ethics That Protects You

Mental health professionals adhere to a strict code of ethics regarding such things as keeping your conversations with them confidential and respecting your rights as an individual. This code applies to those who see you if you are hospitalized in a mental health facility as well.

> CONFIDENTIALITY BROKEN: *There was a slip in the confidentiality prior to my first appointment. I asked not to be contacted at home, and yet a letter confirming my appointment was sent to my home address. The office has apologized to me, but the error should not have been made in the first place.*

Laws That Protect You

This section is written as a general guide. Neither of the authors is a lawyer, although an attorney has been consulted for this section. If you feel you need legal advice regarding your therapy, it is strongly advisable for you to discuss your particular situation with your own attorney from your own state. Each state has its own specific laws, and it is important that you are aware of your state's requirements if you are considering legal action against your therapist.

There are laws that protect patients. Anything about your patient record must be kept in confidence by your therapist. Disciplinary action can be instituted against any mental health professional who does not comply with the law, and lawsuits can be filed. A therapist can also be disciplined by the institution that licensed her or the professional association of which she is a member.

If a therapist violates your confidentiality, for example, or makes sexual advances toward you, you could appeal to any or all of these three bodies: the legal system, the licensing institution or the appropriate professional association.

The Court System

Most states have laws or recorded decisions that prevent psychiatrists, psychologists and social workers from producing client records and testifying in court about client consultation and/or correspondence. The U.S. Supreme Court ruled in *Jaffee v. Redmond* (June 13, 1996) to grant "extended privilege" (that is, protection from federal court subpoena or court order) to confidential communications between psychotherapists and their clients. (Psychotherapists are defined as licensed psychiatrists, psychologists and social workers.)[1] These laws recognize a therapist-patient privilege. It is important for you to understand that this does not include a therapist who is *not* a licensed psychologist, psychiatrist or social worker (e.g., pastoral counselor or marriage/family counselor).

However, a court order signed by a judge can override the confidentiality regulations.

Waivers

Just as when you visit your medical doctor, there may be forms you are asked to sign when first seeing a mental health professional. This will depend in part on whether you are seeing a therapist in private practice, an employee assistance program (EAP), or someone made available through an agency or clinic. Read and make sure you understand all these forms before signing them. The forms typically consist of the following:

Insurance forms. These are fairly straightforward and are similar to the ones you would fill out when seeing a physician. There are, however, caps on mental health coverage that are different from limits on physical care. For example, caps for substance abuse treatment may be different from those for physical or other mental health care. Check with your own insurance company; you may have more coverage than you think. Become fully informed of your insurance limitations *before* starting therapy. (See chapter 7 for more information on paying for therapy and applying for insurance benefits.)

Release of information. There are different types of releases. Your therapist may ask you to sign a release that allows her to discuss your case with another expert in the field, such as an ongoing consultant, or to send you to another professional (i.e., provide a referral).

A medical release is a onetime release to see an outside professional, usually a physician or other therapist, for a second opinion or to inform him of your mental health care. If you sign a medical referral, it should be much shorter in duration (one to four weeks).

If you are seeing a therapist because you failed a drug test at work or for some other reason that is job related, you may want to sign a release so your therapist can inform your supervisor that you are getting help in overcoming your problem. Such a release should be subject-specific, the person to be consulted should be specified and the duration of the release limited to no more than six months.

Statement of understanding. On your first interview at an EAP, clinic, nonprofit agency or group practice, this additional form may be included in your records. This form is important for several reasons: It informs you of your rights, what your insurance company is financially responsible for and what stipulations there are regarding restrictions on confidentiality.

Your Records

You have a right to read and copy your records at any time. Do not be afraid to ask *where* they will be kept (they should be in a locked file that only your therapist has access to) as well as *what* they will contain (they should contain the clinician's notes and relevant forms). Ask if anyone else will be able to see them. If the receptionist is allowed access, you can ask for a signed confidentiality agreement from him. Also, when therapy starts, discuss the therapist's policy for ultimately destroying your records. Insist that she keep them no longer than one year after you end therapy. If the therapist closes her practice, be sure to inform her that you want your records destroyed. The time frame legally mandated for each profession may differ, but you can at least insist on a plan.

> *DR. MASI LEARNS A LESSON: One day I received a letter from a psychologist I'd never met, introducing himself and informing me that he was taking over the practice of a previous therapist whom I had seen years ago who had died. He stated that he'd read my records and was available for any type of treatment I might need. Angry at the violation of my privacy, I immediately arranged for the destruction of the records.*

Tape-Recorded Sessions

Some therapists prefer to tape-record sessions so they will not be distracted by writing notes. Whether you feel comfortable with this is obviously a very personal decision. You may want to find out who will be transcribing the tapes, when they will be destroyed and where they will be kept. If you agree to tape-recorded sessions, ask for a signed statement *from the therapist* that details this procedure.

You may also want to tape-record your sessions. By all means ask your therapist. He may or may not agree.

Contracts

You may feel comfortable having a contract with your builder, child-care provider or car mechanic. It is perfectly appropriate to do the same with your therapist—therapy is a substantial investment. A therapist/client contract is best utilized in short-term relationships when both parties agree to certain things during a specified period of time: for example, the number of sessions, topics to be discussed, contact information, follow-up, finances, date of conclusion, etc.

Contact Information

Make sure the therapist has numbers and addresses that you can use to reach her during the workday, evenings and on weekends. You may have an emergency that would necessitate speaking to her during off hours. Many therapists will actually telephone you if they have not heard from you for a while or are concerned about your emotional health. If you do not want the therapist to call or write to you at home or work, be sure to make this perfectly clear from the outset.

She should honor your request. You can also ask that you always be the one to call the therapist.

> *HELPED WITH FOLLOW-UP: Janice J. was very persistent in following up on my progress. Initially, I found this to be somewhat of an irritant, but it proved to be exactly what I needed.*

When the Confidentiality Code Can Be Broken

You should be aware of the major exceptions to client confidentiality and when it can be broken.

A court order. A court order signed by a judge can override the confidentiality regulations.

Harm to yourself. If the therapist has reason to believe that you are about to harm yourself, he can take appropriate steps to protect you.

Harm to children. In all cases of suspected child abuse or neglect, the therapist has a legal duty to report this to the appropriate state agency. A therapist who fails to do this may be vulnerable to criminal and civil prosecution.

Harm to others. If the therapist believes you will harm others, as in cases of elder abuse, domestic violence or stalking, the therapist has a duty to warn whoever is designated by your state. This is usually a social service agency or the police.

Acts of terrorism. If a client discloses plans to kidnap someone, take a hostage or bomb property, the therapist has a duty to warn the appropriate authorities.

Accrediting bodies, inspections and audits. If your record is held by a program or hospital, it can be reviewed by

bona fide evaluators for purposes of compliance with professional standards. The Joint Commission on Accrediting of
Healthcare Organizations (JCAHO) is an example of such an
accrediting body.

4

THE CHOICE IS YOURS
Researching the Profession

Sometimes it can seem that everyone today is calling herself some type of therapist. How can you get through the quagmire without taking too much time and expending unnecessary energy? We have summarized the most important qualifications you should look for in order to select the best "fit" for you. Be warned, however: Not every "Dr." is qualified to be your therapist!

> *A PH.D. IN QUESTION: During a review Dale asked to see the résumé of Dr. J. due to the poor nature of his clinical work. When she saw the résumé, she understood. His Ph.D. was in history!*

An already saturated marketplace is seeing the number of mental health professionals mushrooming: An increase of 25 percent is estimated over the next several years. In 1997 there were 394,800 mental health professionals working in America. Of these, 33,000 were psychiatrists; 70,000 were doctoral psychologists; 189,000 were clinically trained social workers; 50,000 were licensed professional counselors; 46,000 were marriage and family counselors; and 6,800 were certified mental health nurse specialists.[1] Massachusetts tops the chart with over 228 mental health professionals for every 100,000 citizens. For New York the figure was 156.8, and for California it was 138.5. Mississippi is at the bottom of the list, with only 32.1 professionals for every 100,000 citizens.[2]

Interestingly, while there is approximately one mental health professional for every 1,000 Americans, most HMO mental health programs rely on merely one mental health clinician for every *5,000 to 6,000* members. As Americans continue to drift into such organized systems of care, there could be a surplus of as many as 80,000 to 100,000 licensed mental health professionals across the country.[3] The pressure on mental health clinicians who want to stay in business is very intense. How can you work through this thickening maze of selections and specialties to find the best match for you?

Do you want to know how most people do it? According to Dr. Kenneth Kessler, CEO of the former managed behavioral health care company American PsychManagement (now ValueOptions), they use the telephone book. Think about how strange this is. Would you rely on advertisements in the Yellow Pages to choose your child's nanny or your physician? Even your car mechanic? Learning about the different kinds of therapists out there, the type of education they have pursued and the experiences they have is smarter (and safer!) than letting your fingers do the walking.

You have a great deal of control in selecting your therapist. These days, therapy is a buyer's market, particularly if you have health insurance or private funds to cover the cost. Many private therapists have lost a lot of clients—and income—as managed care programs tighten the mental health benefits they offer. More than ever, therapists are competing for clients, so take a little time to shop around.

Many insurance plans may not reimburse fees paid to "alternative" therapists such as masseurs, acupuncturists and counselors with certain types of graduate degrees or degrees from certain nonaccredited institutions. These types of therapists are not discussed here, although their methods are described in the appendix. In any case, be sure to confirm that your insurance company will pay for your therapist *before* you start your formal sessions.

The finest therapists are the ones who keep abreast of new developments. The mental health field itself is more sophisticated than ever, with specialties in such focused areas as addiction, depression and eating disorders. There are myriad types of methodological approaches to counseling, from cognitive to brief therapy. If a therapist you are thinking of seeing says that she can "treat anything," put up your guard. Having a proven expertise is probably one of the most important factors to look for in choosing a good therapist. Not even the brightest, most caring therapist can claim expertise in all specialties and all methods.

Those Who Provide Therapy

Marriage and Family Therapists

A marriage and family counselor should have a master's degree in marriage and family therapy, with two years of supervised clinical training. Some states do not require a license or clinical training.

Mental-Health Counselors

A mental-health counselor should have a master's degree in mental health, 3,000 hours of clinical experience and supervised clinical work. They are also licensed in some states. According to Michael Lane, consultant to American Mental Health Counselors' Association (AMHCA), "there are seven states that do not currently require state licensure for mental health counselors."[4] The seven states are Connecticut, New York, Pennsylvania, Alaska, Indiana, Minnesota, and Nevada. If you are in one of these states, it is strongly advised that you carefully check the credentials of any prospective mental-health counselor.

Nurse Clinician

This is a licensed profession. A nurse clinician should have a master of science (M.S.) degree in nursing. He should also have certification from the American Nurses Association as a psychiatric mental health clinical specialist and be licensed as a registered nurse (R.N.).

Pastoral Counselor

This profession is licensed in some states. In addition, a pastoral counselor may have a license to practice therapy under the auspices of another professional group. This type of therapist should be able to show evidence of advanced training in the area of pastoral counseling. She typically has a religious perspective in terms of therapy and change. Members of the clergy often have advanced training as pastoral counselors.

Psychiatrist

A psychiatrist is not only licensed as a medical physician, but also has studied the treatment of mental illness for an additional number of years (usually four). The psychiatrist should also be board certified in his profession. A psychiatrist can prescribe medication.

Psychoanalysts

Psychoanalysts are required to have a master's degree, four years training in a training institute recognized by the National Association for the Advancement of Psychoanalysis (NAAP), hundreds of hours of personal individual psychoanalysis, seminar attendance and psychoanalytic case supervision. The practicing psychoanalyst should also have certification with the NAAP, although this is not required. This discipline was popular in the 1960s and 1970s, but is less so now, due to the high costs involved with the number of daily sessions necessary for significant progress.

Psychologist

This is a licensed profession. The psychologist has obtained a doctorate in psychology, designated as a Ph.D. or Psy.D. When reviewing his qualifications, check for clinical experience as opposed to research or testing. The psychologist typically has extensive experience in behavioral testing. He will often use psychological testing as part of the diagnostic process.

Social Worker

This is a licensed profession. The licensed social worker has successfully completed a two-year program in the study of social work. Some go on to attain the highest degree in the field, which is a master of social work (M.S.W.). Although some schools of social work do offer a doctoral program, a doctorate is not necessary to obtain a license to practice.

Credentials

The three primary credentials for you to be aware of are graduate degree, license and area of expertise.

To practice, your mental health professional should have:

- A graduate degree from an accredited university in one of the mental health professions. Numbers of schools are springing up, particularly with "distance education," that do not have accreditation. Supervised clinical training should have been part of your therapist's education. This is very important. For example, some therapists with a master's degree in counseling and psychology may not have internship experience.

- A state license. Licensing provides the public with some accountability, as each state has a system for disciplining and adjudicating mental health professionals accused of violating the state's code of professional behavior.[5] State licensure varies greatly by state, but certainly is desirable. Some mental health professionals do not have a license to practice. Yet they have many clients. Practicing without a license is not illegal in many states but is fraught with hazards for the client.

• Experience and training in your area of need.

Types of Therapists

There are eight primary mental health disciplines. You will find that the minimum academic requirements, clinical training schedules and licensure that are presented are the basic criteria for each discipline. The disciplines are certified pastoral counselors, certified social workers, marriage and family therapists, mental health counselors, psychiatrists, psychoanalysts and psychologists.

A good therapist should also belong to the professional association to which his field relates and have at least five years of experience in the type of problem with which you are grappling. Also look for one who has earned credits from continuing education and carries malpractice insurance.

Area of Expertise

This is by far the most important category for you to consider in your search for the best therapist for your needs. By now you should have a sense of the issues you would like to work through in therapy. You may also have the primary and secondary issues you would like your therapist to address and therefore have experience in. You may hear a therapist say that he has seen all kinds of problems in years spent in private practice and that this qualifies him for treating all types of issues. Just because a therapist has experience in treating one type of mental health problem does not mean that he is qualified to treat others.

> *DISSATISFIED WITH THERAPIST'S EXPERTISE: When I called the office, it was clear to me that marriage counseling was required. My first session with Dr. J. only confirmed that. Dr. J.'s specialty is not marriage counseling. The bottom line is that my sessions were a waste of time.*

Experience in the specific area you need help with is often the most relevant guideline to follow when choosing a therapist. Take addictions as an example. Presently, there is no special coursework in addiction required for all students attending professional schools of mental health (e.g., psychiatry, psychology, social work). Most consumers would find this surprising. This situation means that the experience the therapist has had treating clients with addiction is all the more relevant, and an extremely important consideration if you, your partner or another family member suffers from an addiction.

> *AN ADDICTION CASE: My counselor claimed to specialize in substance abuse, but as we went on, I began to feel that she knew nothing about recovery and the personality of an alcoholic. I felt I had to explain myself to her. That was the last thing I needed.*

Take your teenager's depression as another example of the importance in finding a therapist with the right specialization. A marriage counselor who has proved invaluable to you and your spouse may not necessarily be the best person to treat a depressed teen. Your teenager would be better served with a therapist who has at least five years of experience dealing with your child's specific age group. It is important to remember this, despite the fact that you have no doubt learned to trust and believe in your therapist, given the help she has provided for you and your spouse.

If you are a member of a minority group, gay or lesbian, or physically challenged, it may be important for you to have a therapist with a similar background. Do not be afraid to ask for certain preferences, and trust your instincts about biases a therapist seems to have. Gender can be another important consideration, especially for women who have been sexually abused or harassed, are experiencing fertility problems, have gender-associated illnesses such as breast or ovarian cancer, or have been the victim of incest. Many well-meaning male therapists think they can work effectively with female victims of rape and incest as well as other gender-specific issues. Despite the best of intentions, however, the odds of this being true are so small that selecting only female therapists for certain problems and situations is often the wisest route. Conversely, a male therapist may be more appropriate for a man dealing with power issues, sexual difficulties or gender-specific health issues such as prostate cancer.

> *HELPED BY THERAPIST'S COMMON GROUND: I found my therapist, Larry L., to be knowledgeable in many areas. I found he was able to identify with my particular situations concerning work, marriage and religion. So I feel we made a connection that was really able to help me. And I think that it's important when you have a feeling of hopelessness to be able to at least reach out to someone who can identify with some of your feelings.*

Résumé

Most therapists keep a résumé and will share it with you. Don't be shy about requesting one during an interview or about asking some general background questions pertaining to a therapist's work experience and education. This will help you determine not only how effective the therapist is likely to be in your area of need, but also the types of facilities where he has practiced and how long he has been working. It will also give you knowledge of his credentials.

Consider the experience of the following therapists:

- Gwen, a licensed social worker, has been practicing in a psychiatric hospital for twenty years and has decided to go into private practice.
- Kenneth has been in private practice for many years, but has not done any work in your area of need.
- Beth is fresh out of graduate school, newly licensed and has only seen clients under strict clinical supervision.

You probably would not want Kenneth or Beth as your therapist, but without being informed, you could easily end up with one of them. However, Gwen could be ideal due to her extensive work with severely mentally ill patients and her energy and enthusiasm for starting a new practice. There are many aspects to a therapist's career that will remain unknown to you unless your questions are specific.

Certification/Credentialing

When interviewing a therapist, you may be told that he is certified by a particular agency or association. This means that in the eyes of that agency or association, the therapist has met certain predetermined professional qualifications. Fulfilling certification requirements is an excellent way for therapists to continue to get experience and education in their area of expertise, but be sure to ask about the organization that is offering the certification, and that organization's requirements, before blindly accepting the endorsement. The Employee Assistance Professional Association (EAPA), for example, is an organization that grants the title of Certified Employee Assistance Professional (CEAP) to those who have demonstrated that they have at least three years of experience in the EAP field and have scored adequately on a series of exams. However, it is not the same as a license to practice therapy.

Tread carefully. The mental health industry has seen some scams, with nonprofessional bodies declaring therapists "board-certified providers" only because they have paid a fee to attend a seminar.

Logistics: Malpractice Insurance, Lawsuits, Past Charges

There are therapists who have had malpractice lawsuits filed against them, lost their insurance and continue to practice. Ask any prospective therapist about her current malpractice insurance. Therapists who do not carry this type of insurance are either naive or, possibly, ineligible to practice. It certainly throws into question the therapist's competence as a professional. It is important that the therapist have malpractice insurance so that if you were ever to file a lawsuit, you could reach a financial settlement with her insurance company. You may feel awkward or intrusive asking about this, wanting to avoid the impression of being a person who readily sues. Express this concern to the therapist, and explain why you are asking.

If the therapist reacts negatively to the subject overall—dismissing the need to show you evidence of her insurance, for example—you have actually gained an important piece of information: a sense of her accountability to clients.

> *DR. MASI SPEAKS OUT: As a professor in a social work school, I am deeply troubled that the organization responsible for accrediting social work schools— the Council on Social Work Education—does not recommend a course in substance abuse or brief counseling (a solution-focused type of therapy where many problems can be resolved in a short time). Mental health professionals and professors often perpetuate methods and practices that are outdated and ineffective. Unless an overseeing body begins to define the best practices for clients seeking therapy by insisting on outcome measurements, therapists can continue to use approaches that are not as effective as some of the more recent ones such as utilizing medication and brief therapy.*

5

A CUSTOM FIT
Interviewing and Selecting Your Therapist

The type of mental health professional you choose—psychologist, social worker, psychiatrist, mental health counselor—is ultimately *your* decision. Try not to let your physician, family members or others influence you in making the selection. In truth, unless you are receiving medication, you may be unable to tell the difference among them at this point. But session rates, methodology and approaches will definitely differ, depending on the type of therapist you choose. However, you may limit your personal choice if you decide to use your insurance benefit.

Finding the Best Therapist for You

Consult your warning signs checklist and action plan as you set out to select a therapist. This will not only save you time and money, but will also give you a measure of clarity and a sense of control. For example, if you are struggling with grief and questioning spiritual issues and mortality, a pastoral counselor may be appropriate. But if you are depressed and need prescription medications, you may also need a psychiatrist. Keep in mind that various types of therapists work with psychiatrists; the psychiatrist manages your medical condition, while the therapist does the counseling. This scenario can work quite well, in addition to cutting costs since you would spend less time with the more costly psychiatrist.

Consider the following suggestions and guidelines as you try to narrow down the choices.

Recommendations and Referrals

Some people find a therapist through recommendations and referrals, and for good reason. It is the most effective approach. Pick individuals you consider able to be objective and honest with you. Filter through their recommendations with your specific needs in mind.

Try asking any mental health professionals you might know for referrals as well. A therapist who has worked with you on a previous problem may have worked with someone who he feels is better qualified to work with you now. Nonprofit agencies focused on your area of need can also be excellent resources. Family services, rape crisis centers, battered women's shelters and your EAP are just a few examples. There are also referral resource organizations that list groups and agencies organized by subject. Check the Yellow Pages in your local telephone book for the names of such organizations. Be sure this is not your sole source for finding a therapist.

Surprisingly, professional associations, such as the American

Association for Marriage and Family Therapy, will *not* refer you to a therapist. Their function is to set up guidelines for professional qualifications in your particular state. Referrals from your physician can also be tricky. Many are most comfortable referring you to another medical doctor—a psychiatrist—but that may not be the type of therapist you need most.

Your Insurance Company's List of Providers

Insurance companies will send you a list of the mental health providers that your policy covers. If you decide to select a therapist this way, start by calling the insurance company and asking them to review with you the types of therapists who specialize in your area of need, and who work close to where you live or spend the day. Sometimes an insurance brochure will also break down the therapists by specialty. With a list in hand, start calling the therapists' offices and filter out several choices with the help of the checklist for researching potential therapists appearing later in this chapter. If you belong to an HMO, you may have to go through your primary care physician to obtain a referral to a therapist. If your physician tries to dissuade you from seeing a therapist, hold firm to your decision. You may have to become your own best advocate as you search for quality specialized care.

If you are in an HMO or restrictive managed care plan, you may have difficulty in obtaining the names of therapists to interview. An HMO may insist that your primary care physician first determine your need for therapy. A restrictive managed care program may not agree that you need therapy. Your options may include going to your human resource department or EAP, who can be an advocate for you with the insurance company or managed care company.

Your Employer's Employee Assistance Program (EAP)

An employee assistance program (EAP) is a professional assessment, referral and/or short-term counseling service offered to employees with problems that may be affecting their jobs. Employees either contact the EAP when they wish to do so or when they are referred to the EAP by their supervisors.

If your employer has an EAP, you should consider using it as a resource first, unless you have reason to question its competency. According to the Employee Assistance Professional Association, more than twenty thousand companies had EAPs as of 1995. These programs, which are free to the employee and, in some cases, family members, can serve as excellent resources for all types of mental health care needs. Most employers contract an EAP provider for a maximum of six to eight sessions for each employee in a calendar year. If you need long-term care, the EAP will not only help you find a referral resource, but may also be able to provide guidance in paying for the referral.

A word of caution. Some EAP professionals have little mental health or substance abuse training. Even though the counselor may tell you that she is a certified employee assistance professional (CEAP), this does not guarantee that she has ever seen a patient. Ask the prospective EAP practitioner to be specific about the type of background that she has, and make sure that it matches the type of help you need.

Nonprofit Agencies

Nonprofit agencies can be another important resource. Because of their size, they have access to a large pool of therapists with a broad base of training and expertise. If you have a range of issues or family members to be seen, they can be excellent places to get the full spectrum of therapy you need in one place. In addition, they often have support groups, staff training and in-house psychiatrists and psychologists for medication and testing. If you do not like one particular therapist, you can also ask for a referral to another within the same agency.

Community Resources and the United Way

If you have limited finances, explore your community for resources. Family service associations, religious charities and a myriad of other programs are excellent places to find individual and group therapy, child and family therapy, and support groups. Although they usually choose a therapist for you, most such agencies will try hard to find somebody appropriate for your needs. Communities vary greatly in the number and range of resources they have. Contact the United Way group in your community for guidance in finding the agency that will best meet your needs.

The Next Step: The Initial Phone Call

You should now have a list of potential therapists. Ideally, you would call their offices, weed out those who seem inappropriate and set up appointments to meet with two or three before making a final selection. You know you should comparison shop before you buy a car, select a contractor or choose a physician. However, though you may be in the position of deciding to initiate therapy, you may be too emotional or distracted to go through this process. The most important thing is to pick up the phone, make an appointment and see whomever you can. You may need to do a shortened version of the initial process. Once you are in therapy, you may then be able to step back and determine if it is working well for you and make any necessary changes at that point.

> *BEWILDERED AND GRIEVING: My husband passed away less than two months ago, and my loss is horrific. I have never gone through anything like this before. My husband was my best friend, soul mate, lover, father of our six children and the head of our household. How can I, at this time, be objective about anything?*

If you have the time and detachment to shop around, then the next step is to start calling the offices of the therapists from your list. You may be able to obtain a lot of basic information from the receptionist, eliminating a number of choices for obvious reasons, such as wrong area of expertise, gender other than what you wanted or lack of licensing. Most therapists should be willing to speak with you directly, even if the conversation only lasts five to ten minutes and is focused on the therapist's background. Do not use this time to discuss your particular problem in depth. Make sure you get your questions answered. The therapist will also be trying to determine if she is the right type for you.

> *A SATISFIED CLIENT: I was very satisfied with the service I received. Jane helped me to understand my problems and put me back on the road to helping myself. She gave me contacts to get myself and my son on the road to recovery. She talked to me as a person who truly cared about me and my well-being. I will always be grateful to her.*

Researching Potential Therapists Checklist

Use the following checklist to help you choose the best therapist for you.

☐ Location, convenience

☐ Gender

☐ Race

☐ Academic degree and institution from which it was received

☐ State license

☐ Certifications

☐ Malpractice insurance

☐ Area of expertise

☐ Particular school of therapy

☐ Years in private practice since receiving a graduate degree and license

☐ Years of experience in your area of need

☐ Continuing education/training recently attended

☐ Average session rate or fee per hour

☐ Availability of and schedule for appointments

Don't get caught up in having to accommodate a therapist's time. Increasing numbers of therapists are

available for evening and weekend sessions. If you need either, you should be direct and very clear about this. Ultimately, the scheduling should be at a mutually agreeable time.

☐ Length of time of first session
This is often longer than the typical session.

☐ Is there a sliding fee scale?

☐ Typical frequency of sessions
Many therapists like to start out once a week for two or three sessions, then go for longer periods in between, rather than seeing you once every two weeks in the beginning.

IMMEDIATELY TURNED A LIFE AROUND: The day I called I was at the end of the road, ready to call it quits! Everyone was so good; they got me in within an hour of my call. Otherwise I do not think I would have made it through the day. After all the help I have received, I can do a lot better with my life today.

Screening the Candidates

At this point you should have two or three choices for therapists. Armed with your warning signs checklist, action plan and researching potential therapists checklist, you are now ready for the interviewing process or your first visit. You will be expected to pay for this visit since you will be discussing your particular issues, deciding if your personalities will work well together and meeting for a full session (fifty to sixty minutes). Ask ahead of time if the potential candidates will meet with you for a shortened period (twenty to thirty minutes) in order for you to save yourself time and money during this interview process.

Remember that meeting with two or three therapists is an approach to use *only* if you have the time, resources and desire to do so. If your insurance company will only refer you to one therapist, if you have limited finances and cannot shop around or, most important, if you are not interested in or do not feel emotionally equipped to go through an interviewing process, then by all means skip this step and find somebody to immediately help you feel better. You can always use the evaluation system outlined in chapter 8 at a later date to determine if you are going in the right direction. If not, you can then switch your therapist if necessary. If at all possible, however, it is highly recommended that you meet with more than one therapist before entering therapy. It could save you time and money down the road.

The Interview

The interview is different from the first session with your chosen therapist. The interview should include a discussion of your particular issues and deciding if you are comfortable with each other. Make sure the therapist is aware of this—that the first meeting is one in which you want to determine if the two of you can have a productive relationship—and do not be surprised if some will not see you under these circumstances. Many therapists have had only limited experience with clients who carefully shop around. On the other hand, the therapist who is open to and used to this type of encounter will likely utilize it as an opportunity to decide if the two of you can work together as well.

You may be uncomfortable about interviewing a therapist. This is completely normal.

Being on Time

Some disciplines place a great deal of emphasis on having the client arrive on time on a regular basis. If you do not, it may be interpreted as your avoiding issues, being fearful or defensive, not being committed, or not having your heart in the process.

The Setting

It may seem trivial, but until you actually see where the therapy will take place, it is difficult to determine if it is a comfortable place for you to discuss your feelings. Do not question yourself if an office doesn't feel right; simply move on to the next therapist on your list.

> *WOULDN'T WORK FOR SOME: One of Dale's reviewers was visiting a prospective therapist to check on her credentials and found the office had incense burning, no chairs—only pillows for seating—and Indian music playing in the background. Another example was of a therapist's office located in her home. This is often the case for therapists in private practice and, if handled appropriately, can be a nice option. However, in this case it was necessary to climb over children's toys and greet the family before entering the office.*

It is never appropriate for you to meet family when seeing a therapist in her home. In addition, you may not wish to see a therapist in her home due to the personal element it brings into the relationship. Being aware of these preferences is important and perfectly appropriate.

> *A SATISFIED CLIENT: The therapist's office is very receptive to schedules and changes. They try to maintain privacy when I enter and leave. I appreciate it.*

What to Expect

You find the office, have arrived on time or even a little early and are ready for a face-to-face meeting. What happens? The therapist may have a nurse or receptionist greet you and give you the necessary papers to register you with the practice. Or the therapist may greet you and have you fill out the forms before beginning the session. Either way, the therapist should warmly greet you, shake your hand and invite you into her office to sit down. The most common furniture arrangement is several comfortable chairs facing each other. There are usually no couches in therapists' offices unless they are to sit on. Therapists do not usually sit behind a desk unless they are taking notes.

The Greeting

As trivial as it may sound, how is the therapist addressing you? Does the therapist refer to you as "Mr.," "Mrs." or "Ms.," and do you refer to the therapist as the same or as "Dr."? Or does the therapist refer to you by your first name and you refer to the therapist as "Dr."? Does the therapist refer to you as a "client" or a "patient"? This charged language immediately sets up a difference in power that may not be the optimal way to begin your relationship.

Logistical Issues in Therapy

Get the Facts About Your Area of Need

In this initial one-on-one interview, most therapists should be able to give you a rough idea of how many clients he has treated in your particular area of need. Ask any questions you did not have a chance to pose during the first telephone call.

Negotiating a Fee

If you can promise a potential therapist a certain number of sessions over a set period of time, he may be willing to negotiate a lower per-session rate. Many therapists charge on a sliding scale to accommodate people with limited resources. However, you usually have to ask to find out about this.

The Interview Checklist

At the end of your interview, you should be able to answer most of the following.

☐ Do your schedules coincide?

_____

_____

☐ Does he accept your insurance, and how does he expect you to pay for each session?

_____

_____

☐ How long is a session?

_____

_____

☐ What is the fee?

_____

_____

☐ What happens in an emergency? Can he be reached easily?

_____

_____

☐ Can he be reached on weekends or holidays?

_____

_____

☐ Who does he use for backup?

_____

_____

☐ Is he part of a group of therapists?

_____

_____

☐ Is he available for telephone consultation between sessions? Is there a fee?

_____

_____

☐ Who does he use to prescribe medication (if applicable)?

_____

_____

☐ How many hours of supervision/training does he receive per month?

_____

_____

☐ What happens if you are late?

_____

_____

☐ What happens if you cancel a session? Do you need to do this within twenty-four hours to avoid paying for a scheduled session?

_____

_____

☐ What about vacations—yours and the therapist's?

_____

_____

> *A FRUSTRATED CLIENT: Jane was forty-five minutes late for our appointment. Previously, we had decided I needed another therapist more experienced in my area of need. She said she would have a referral for me the next day. She did not respond, and after a week I had to call her for the referral.*

Making the Decision

Would you buy the first car you test-drive? Hire the first nanny you interview to take care of your child? Probably not. Apply the same caution to your mental health. Hold off on making a decision until you have met more than one candidate. It is appropriate to tell the therapist that you are talking to others as well.

> *A DISAPPOINTED CLIENT: I'm sure the therapist is a good person and helps many with their problems, but I left feeling I had gotten nowhere. I don't think she understood that I never would have been there if I wasn't really troubled. In fifty-one years I never asked for help before. But I will not be returning; it just didn't work for me.*

Interviewing the therapists can be quite challenging. After the first session, particularly if you are new to therapy, you may feel somewhat better, lighter, more optimistic about your situation. After all, you have just discussed your problems with a professional who may have provided some very useful input. Unfortunately, the afterglow of the initial interview may not reappear after the second, third or even the fourth session. This may be due to the depth of your problems or to the therapist's skill. Differences among therapists can be quite subtle. If it is feasible, both emotionally and financially, try to see at least two therapists before deciding on one.

> *A DISCOURAGED CLIENT: Steve seemed very tired (bored?) most of the time. He had a hard time concentrating on our conversations and stifled many yawns. Sometimes I felt his sincerity wasn't really there.*

Do not start seeing a therapist who:

- Makes you feel unsafe, intimidated or frightened
- Refuses to answer your initial questions, particularly relating to her background and experience
- Resists considering problems or subjects that you feel are notable or important
- Labels you with a diagnosis that seems extreme

> *AN EMPTY-HANDED CLIENT: I looked for another therapist after my first meeting with Jim because I felt he didn't understand how agitated I felt at the time and he didn't give me any reading material or anything more positive than one "mind-over-matter" exercise to do. I felt I needed more.*

A Final Check-In

Finally, consider the logistical and financial details. Can you set up appointments with little difficulty in scheduling? Is the fee going to work out for your budget based on how long the therapist feels you need to work on the primary issues you have noted in your action plan? Can you commit to the length of time recommended by the therapist? Remember, this may be longer than your original assessment. As the client, you should ask yourself, *Does this counselor have not only the skills that will allow me to open up and discover things, but also give me a feeling of hope?*

> AN UNIMPRESSED CLIENT: *The doctor was well versed in his field but did not seem to have much interest in me as an individual. At times when I spoke, he seemed not to be listening and would then turn around and ask questions about what I had just given him answers to. Each session he would keep looking at my papers, shaking his head and saying, "Boy, this is weird insurance."*

The Choice Is Yours

After meeting with *preferably* two therapists, you have gathered enough information to make an informed choice. Feel confident in your choice because you have made it methodically and knowledgeably. Again, remember that if you decide to enter the process with your first contact, the most important thing is for you to start therapy. Don't worry, even if you've interviewed several, if the person is or is not a perfect "fit." It will become evident along the way.

Do not start therapy until you (and the therapist) have a concrete idea of what the relationship entails. One of the biggest problems in therapy is that the client ends up feeling like he is not making progress, and at a steep cost. Focused goals established at the outset, and periodic progress check-ins, can greatly help to alleviate this dynamic.

Conversely, if you have interviewed three or four therapists and have been dissatisfied with all of them, you may want to

take a look in the mirror and consider the possibility that your
demands are too extreme. Chances are that something going
on inside of you is holding you back from starting therapy.

Therapists rarely refuse clients. Remember, this is their
livelihood. Unless you have a very unusual case or problems
completely out of the therapist's range of expertise, he will
likely accept you as a client. It is up to *you* to decide if the
relationship will work for you. Do not look to the therapist to
make this decision. You are the client—the customer, the
buyer—and should select the most appropriate person for
your needs.

> *GLAD TO HAVE MADE THE DECISION TO SEEK
> THERAPY: I cannot say enough about Lauren's pro-
> fessionalism and expertise. She was upbeat, cheerful,
> and always pleasant and supportive. It was initially
> a very difficult decision to seek help, but she made me
> feel comfortable immediately, and there was instant
> rapport. She helped me enormously, and I'll miss our
> "conversations."*

6

A TYPICAL SESSION
What Happens in Therapy?

You've selected a therapist who seems a good "fit." You are now ready to buckle down and get to work. What happens in a typical session? How will you know what to expect, if it's going "normally" or even "well"? If you've never been in therapy—and may be fearful of what happens—here's a snapshot of what usually occurs.

The First Session

During this first visit, you and the therapist will be discussing your problem in detail. He may take a comprehensive personal history, or you may discuss a particular crisis that brought you in. You should be doing most of the talking, particularly in the first thirty to forty minutes. The therapist may or may not take notes. He will likely take the last fifteen to twenty minutes to summarize what you have said, and perhaps offer a diagnosis and a suggested course of treatment.

To begin the process there are typically three scenarios:

1. You are overwhelmed with a particular issue/crisis and want to discuss the problem before any type of formal interaction is begun. The therapist deals with your present feelings and your emotional reaction to help you calm down, feel better, and find a solution. From there she will ask more questions to get a context for the situation and some background on you and your family.

2. She may be aware of the particular problem/issue you've come to discuss and will ask you the history of that problem, how long you've been feeling this way, and other questions about the particular problem and the circumstances surrounding it.

3. If you have no particular pressing crisis, the therapist may start with a personal history. If you are uneasy, nervous and even a little tongue-tied, this is a good way to get to know more about you. At this point, particular issues that are relevant to why you are there usually come out.

The progression and content of the first few sessions largely depend upon *you* and your condition when you come through the door. If you are in a crisis, the emphasis will be on that particular issue with no personal history taken until perhaps the second or third session. If not, a personal history may be taken right away and, most often, several pertinent issues to focus on arise from it.

If you are not in a crisis situation, the beginning of the first or second session is the time to bring up the goals set in your action plan. You will find most therapists will welcome your organized approach. You've clearly thought through your issues and reasons for seeking therapy. This makes the process run more smoothly and makes it much easier to work through from both perspectives—yours and the therapist's.

Almost every therapist will begin the first session with why you are in therapy *now*. From there he will usually follow your train of thought, depending on where you start, and may look for other issues. Ideally, the therapist should join you along your trail, rather than lead the way. In reality, the therapist's responsibility to your insurance provider may also determine some of the questions and paths taken in the process.

There should be a balance between the therapist's talking and leading in the process and your doing the same. The best therapy is a balance between being helped and giving you room to present issues at your own pace.

Some early questions asked by the therapist may be:

- Why are you here today?
- Is there anything in particular that is troubling you?
- What is your personal history (marital status, health, job, relationships, etc.)?
- What is your family history?
- Are you aware of any dysfunction or unusual experiences in your childhood?

Personal History

You may be asked your marital status, if you have children, the type of work you do, where you attend(ed) school, your educational status, your living arrangement, if you are living close to your family of origin, your health status and other questions related to your personal life.

Family History

The therapist will ask you questions about key members in your family of origin, their roles in your development and if you are living near them. He will ask if there is any substance abuse or mental illness in the family, if anybody close to you had a chronic or terminal illness or was suicidal, or if there were other catastrophic events that may have occurred in your childhood. Illness histories will be taken on your care-givers and siblings.

Use of Screens

Depending on the problem(s) you want to discuss, the therapist may ask you to rate yourself using an instrument or written test, called a screen. A screen is comprised of questions that are targeted to produce a specific diagnosis, such as substance abuse or depression. (See the appendix for more information about screens.) Some therapists also use the Myers-Briggs Type Indicator (MBTI), which is more of a personality or character analysis. If it makes you feel more comfortable, speak with the therapist first about the specific instrument she is recommending and what it will illuminate. The therapist should *always* share the results with you.

Special Advice for Newcomers

It is particularly important for the newcomer to therapy not to assume the therapist knows more than you do about your situation. You should look to be treated as an equal from the very beginning of the relationship in order to maintain as much control as possible over the process. Keep asking for help if you're having trouble communicating or getting ideas across, or if you feel confused. Keep believing you have a *right* to get help.

Appropriate Responses from Newcomers

- I've never done this before.
- I'm not ready to talk about that right now.
- Tell me more about why you are asking that.
- Tell me what you are looking for.
- Could you make that question (e.g., "How do you feel about your mother?") more specific?
- Could you ask that another way to help me understand?
- My mind is blank.
- Tell me more about what you want to know, and I'll think about it this week and get back to you next session.

It is perfectly appropriate to take out pencil and paper and take notes. Always feel free to bring up anything!

Emotional Issues and Personal Preferences in Therapy

Be Yourself

This is your time. Many clients try to perform on some level during therapy—either by trying to guess what the therapist wants to hear or by trying to outsmart her. Try to genuinely be yourself.

In addition, if you feel judged, fearful or uncomfortable, by all means bring it up—often the therapist does not know she is bringing this out. Transference is the dynamic that occurs when the therapist becomes the receptor for you to recreate some of your feelings from your family and history. It is completely normal and a natural element of the process.

Learn to Look Within

The most useful therapy tries to help you change your behavior *inside* rather than out (i.e., trying to make your spouse stop drinking, trying to control your teenager's aggressive behavior, etc.). Therapy works better to change what is under our internal, rather than external, control—and what is in our power to change is often the most effective route to feeling better.

Confrontation

In a good therapy relationship there will be confrontations—normal, responsible and healthy ones. Good therapy can go through the process and come out the other side. Bad therapy is when the client feels he has done something wrong by confronting the therapist.

Silences

A good therapist needs to know when to be silent, but not to the point of causing you great discomfort. Long-term psychotherapy uses long silences in the belief that the unconscious needs to emerge in the process. If this is a belief of yours and you think it will help, then use it. If it makes you uncomfortable and you do not prefer to work this way, tell your therapist.

A Therapist, Not a Friend

You may be inclined to choose a therapist with a personality much like that of your best friend. This is not uncommon, but remember you are not in therapy to find another friend. A good therapist will be tough at times, and even confront you if necessary. He should be able to point out destructive patterns or behaviors. Ideally, a therapist is warm, and has excellent listening skills and a sense of humor but is also able to challenge you without generating hostility. The psychiatrist in the film *Good Will Hunting*, played by Robin Williams, aptly portrays the approach of using tough confrontation when necessary but then offering warmth and affection when appropriate.

Many people do not understand the difference between therapy and friendship. A good friendship is an equal partnership—with both individuals talking about and listening to each other's experiences, and offering advice or support. In a friendship, you can expect both of you to talk and listen—and you both get help. In therapy, however, not only does your therapist have the education and experience that qualifies her to give you professional advice and support, she should be getting her emotional help elsewhere—not from you. This is your time to get professional help, and the focus should be on you.

HELPED BY BEING CONFRONTED: Leila was exceptional. She is, from my perspective, a competent professional who quickly went to the root cause of the problem, understood it and helped me begin to deal with it. She was the first mental health professional I have seen (I have seen four others over the past twenty years) who listened for the depth of my situation and didn't listen to my crap.

Cultural Issues

There are cultural issues that define each and every one of us, no matter what our upbringing. These can be manifested in subtle areas, like voice level, hand gesturing, laughing a lot, or whether or not you are comfortable crying or expressing emotions. Cultural differences between you and your therapist are a very legitimate area to explore in therapy—it is always relevant, no matter what your issue. The therapist should bring this up and should be able to deal with any uncomfortable feelings you may have related to each of your cultural differences.

The Perfect Match

Your preferences for a therapist may change depending on your issue. For example, for a rape, sexual abuse, or gender-specific health or sexual issue, a therapist of the same gender may be preferable. Conversely, if dealing with power issues, a different gender may be appropriate.

Consider your primary priorities in a therapist and stick with them. The bottom line is that you are entitled to have the kind of therapist you want. If you are inexperienced with certain cultural or sexual-orientation issues and do not want to deal with them in your therapy, that is perfectly reasonable. Find another therapist if certain issues come up for you that can get in your way. If there is no choice, it should be brought up in therapy and be open for discussion. Your therapist should be equipped to discuss just about anything. Keep remembering that you are a paying customer and should feel free to talk openly about anything that can help you feel better.

Your Time

Be wary of a therapist who spends your session time discussing his own life experiences, or finds other ways to keep the focus off of you. Therapy is *your* time to explore feelings and behavior. There is no need to reciprocate, as in a friendship. However, a balance here is important. In the past, therapists were trained to never divulge anything about themselves to a client. Today, it has been found to be quite normalizing for a therapist to use examples from his life to illuminate a point.

> *ROBIN'S EXPERIENCE WITH A PERSONALLY RESERVED THERAPIST: I visited a therapist, Nancy, for five sessions. At the beginning of each session, to make myself feel comfortable, I would chat about a few things—the weather, traffic, etc.—and would ask some questions about Nancy's background—where she lived, if she had a family, etc. My questions were met with silence or evasion. I became quite uncomfortable with her lack of willingness to divulge anything about herself and resentful of her expectation that I was to bare my soul.*

Advice

You may also be surprised at—and become frustrated with—your therapist's unwillingness to offer advice. A good therapist should function something like an interpreter, taking the confused or charged language you are speaking and translating it into understandable material that enables *you* to make a decision about changing your behavior or your approach to a situation. A balance of good listening skills,

warmth, sense of humor and ability to confront without generating hostility are the ideal personality traits for a therapist. A therapist should open up possibilities that you may
not even have known you had.

---

*AN AMBIVALENT CLIENT: The therapist was very
neutral. I would have liked for him to take more of a
stand on the issues I was facing. He typically said the
same thing week after week—this is a crisis, it will
take time, don't make any major decisions. He
listened very well, but I was looking for much more
feedback than I got.*

There should be a balance between a therapist having a
body of general knowledge and applying it to each individual
client. You should be able to expect answers to questions—
but don't be put off if sometimes she thinks you should come
up with the answer on your own. Advice is appropriate to
give; however, many therapists may not be willing to offer it.
It can be very frustrating to ask a therapist, "What do you
think?"—only to be met with, "What do *you* think?" Her will-
ingness to offer advice may be an important factor in your
decision about the ideal therapist for you.

Two Different Stances in Therapy

The best therapist should be able to work within both of
the following stances; however, due to most therapists' training it is often difficult to find one skillful in both. You should
be able to get a custom "fit" in your therapy, which can happen within all disciplines.

1. The enabling model. For the most part, the therapist helps you help yourself. There will be times during this process when the therapist will not give advice, in the belief that you should be brought to the answers yourself. This is a more traditional approach.
2. The therapist as coach. She gives advice based on your interaction with her, and you go back and forth with a dialogue discussing the issue.

> *AN AGGRAVATED CLIENT: I have used two different therapists and have been disappointed with both. As counselors, they were not much good. They understood my problems but offered no advice. They listened but would not tell me what to do or give me any guidance.*

Boundaries

Personal life. It is perfectly appropriate to ask personal questions of your therapist and to expect that she should answer within reason. However, the intimacy of your questions may provoke her to ask why you are interested in that particular area. It is also within reason to ask your therapist to attend family functions like weddings, graduations and christenings. Therapists will have different policies on attending. However, if he declines, you should get an answer that makes sense to you.

Sexual. How do you know when your sexual boundaries are being crossed? The bottom line is: when it feels uncomfortable to you. Trust yourself, particularly in this matter. Consult an older mentor—a family member, a minister—and get advice. Never stay in a therapeutic situation that is uncomfortable, particularly in a sexual manner.

When you get a crush on your therapist. This dynamic happens more often than you may think. Therapy is a very intimate relationship—after all, who else sees you at your absolute worst and helps and supports you out of it? Therapy can be a very strong connection and it is very natural for intimacy and sexual feelings to go together. However, if it seems to be interfering with your progress, the subject should be brought up. Your therapist should be equipped to deal with this issue—not put you off or make you feel bad.

Crying/Yelling. Therapists are trained to deal with people's extreme emotions, and you should feel free to yell or cry if you feel like it. If you are crying, there is usually a box of tissues in the office. However, you may not get the type of sympathy or reaction that you may expect. The therapist should be empathetic, but she might not walk over and give you a hug. She may just sit and wait for you to collect yourself. It does not mean she does not care. On the other hand, if you are yelling or crying for an extended period, there may be limits placed on you.

Touching. There are certain rules in therapy that protect both parties regarding the use of touch. If you'd like to be touched on the shoulder or patted when sobbing or upset, just ask. The therapist may or may not comply.

A BEREAVED HUSBAND: My wife died after five years of cancer. I was "stuck" and having great difficulty getting on with my life. The situation was having a major impact on my job performance, not to mention my personal life. Ken B. was very professional and courteous, and he helped me get myself back together. He also worked very well with my medical doctor to consider the physical manifestations of my emotional difficulties.

Other Techniques

With regard to other techniques used in therapy, such as meditation, punching pillows, physical touch or role-playing, you should be given an introduction to the method, told how it can help you in your situation and given the *choice* to do this or not—not told to do it. If you are uncomfortable, don't do it. If you start a technique and you are having discomfort, stop and discuss it. Participate in the technique only if you can see how it may be able to help you. It has to make sense to you in order for it to work.

Session Two: Developing a Treatment Plan

Together with the therapist you've selected, your warning signs checklist and your action plan, you are now ready to jointly develop your treatment plan. Unlike the other tools, this one should be done *with* your therapist. This will be another tool that will help you determine if you are really making headway in therapy. You may decide to wait before sharing your other tools with your therapist, which is perfectly appropriate during the first several sessions. If you are still hesitant after several sessions, you may want to examine why you have misgivings about trusting him with this important personal information.

A treatment plan should consist of the following elements that you and your therapist work out together:

- Goals
- Diagnosis
- Methods used for meeting goals (e.g., talk therapy, role-playing, hypnosis, support group, Twelve-Step meetings, reading)

- Length of treatment
- Proposed termination date

Goals

Check back with your action plan for the goals you determined before seeing your therapist. Discuss them with her and jointly determine if they are still the appropriate issues for both of you to place your focus on.

Diagnosis

If you are using insurance, for billing purposes, the therapist will make a formal diagnosis based on the *Diagnostic and Statistical Manual of Mental Disorders IV (DSM-IVR)*, a manual created by the American Psychiatric Association to catalog mental health disorders. The disorders listed encompass such mental-health conditions as anxiety, mild depression, obsessive-compulsive disorder, paranoia and schizophrenia. Some managed care companies no longer authorize payments for some categories of diagnoses. They now demand a more specific, formal diagnosis based on the *DSM-IVR* criteria. It can be scary to get a formal diagnosis for just feeling bad, but it is very helpful in pinpointing the treatment that will help you to feel better, as well as ensuring that your insurance will help pay for it.

Conversely, be aware that this diagnosis is going on your insurance record for others—besides you and your therapist—to see. Once the insurance form with your diagnosis is sent in to your insurance company, it is entered into their records and often consolidated into a large database of medical records. Access is restricted. However, it is important to realize that your past diagnosis may follow you around when you try to obtain other insurance such as life or disability insurance, or even in a court of law. Carefully consider if you are comfortable receiving a label for feeling bad. If you are not, then take the self-pay option.

> BLESSED WITH A DIAGNOSIS: *For years on and off I have seen therapists in times of crisis. Lisa was very patient and kind. She referred me to Alex. He diagnosed me as bipolar (manic-depressive). You can't imagine my relief at finally being properly diagnosed. I already feel much better and look forward to the rest of my life!*

Proposed Method of Treatment

Once you get a diagnosis, it is important to understand the type of treatment your therapist recommends. By now you should be discussing this during your sessions together. Consider getting a second opinion if the treatment strategy being proposed seems drastic, risky or inappropriately expensive (e.g., shock therapy, recommending that you spend an expensive weekend at an alternative program or an extended period of time with your therapist).

Length of Treatment

The decision to stretch therapy much past the point discussed should be *your* decision. Which session will be your last should be discussed ahead of time so that you have a clear sense of how long you will be making commitments of time and money. It will also enable the therapist to see that you view the process as one with a beginning, middle and end. A clear time line will also encourage focus in therapy. You and your therapist will steer away from subjects that are tangential or irrelevant to those included in your action plan, unless your therapist considers the issue fundamental to your improvement.

Proposed Termination Date

Be wary of a therapist who refuses to estimate how long you will be in therapy together. The therapist should be able to do this when making a diagnosis. This is not an unreasonable request. Often therapists do not offer the information, so it may be up to you to request a termination date with the understanding that some flexibility is required of both of you.

Treatment Plan for Therapy

☐ My goals in therapy are:

_____

_____

☐ My diagnosis is:

_____

_____

☐ My therapist will use the following methods in my treatment:

_____

_____

☐ My therapist and I will discuss my progress on [*date, session #*]:

_____

☐ The length of treatment is:

_____

_____

☐ The proposed date of terminating therapy is: _____

Your treatment plan should be a gauge to check when you are feeling off-course or misguided in therapy.

Session Three: The Connection Is Formed

At this point you should be relatively comfortable in therapy and with the therapist you have chosen. You should feel more relaxed and better about yourself. Are you being listened to? Do you like the way you are being treated? Do you feel that you want to keep coming back? If you don't feel connected or that you can trust this particular therapist at this juncture, and feel that you have really tried, trust your instincts and move on.

Therapy Goes Wrong

Therapy can get off track right from the start when a pre-diagnosis is made based on what was said by you on the telephone or in the first visit and when the therapist doesn't let you direct the process. The therapist ends up with a different agenda, and you feel cheated. Stick with your action plan and check back with your warning signs checklist. Consider showing these tools to your therapist to get her back on track.

Another Important *Shrink to Fit* Tool: Journal Keeping

Writing down your thoughts in a journal after every session may seem tedious and time consuming but often proves to be one of the most important tools for assessing your progress. It may seem hard to believe, but you will likely forget how you felt in earlier sessions and what new insights you had gained. A journal offers a window back in time, giving you a valuable perspective on how you were feeling *in the moment* after each session. It will enable you to chart your own progress and help you recollect what occurred between you and the therapist.

Even if you only write brief notes in list form, take the time to do it. Whether detailed or brief, these thoughts from your perspective can prove incredibly valuable to you later on. Note the topics you discussed, any positive or negative impressions, emotional breakthroughs (powerful insights), and general feelings about the session and your therapist.

The following simple outline may be useful as you continue to build your journal. Consider typing this onto a sheet of paper, copying a pile and filling one out after each session.

Journal Notes

• Date of session

_____

_____

• Mood before session (angry, happy, sad)

_____

_____

• Mood after session (angry, happy, sad)

_____

_____

- Topics discussed

_____

_____

- Breakthroughs

_____

_____

- People discussed

_____

_____

- Observations (for example, issues in your past that have surfaced and need to be explored; problems you had not been aware of that are occurring with an individual)

_____

_____

- Feelings about therapist (satisfied, dissatisfied, angry)

_____

_____

- Overall feeling about therapy (satisfied, dissatisfied)

_____

_____

- Comments

_____

_____

Early Therapy Checklist

After your third session, ask yourself the following questions, responding yes or no to each one.

Yes No

☐ ☐ Did you feel comfortable in the office and where it was located?

☐ ☐ Were you seen on time?

☐ ☐ Were you comfortable with the seating arrangement?

☐ ☐ Did the therapist take a thorough personal and family history?

☐ ☐ Did you find the therapist's note taking unobtrusive? (Or was it distracting? Did she type the notes directly into a computer while you were there or tape-record the session? Did this bother you?)

☐ ☐ Did the therapist focus on what *you* feel are the problem areas?

☐ ☐ If you were in crisis, was it handled to your satisfaction?

☐ ☐ Did the therapist discuss your strengths?

☐ ☐ Did the therapist ask follow-up questions to get a clearer sense of what you are going through? (Or did he seem to gloss over most of the issues you presented?)

☐ ☐ Would you rate the therapist as a good listener? Did you feel that she focused on you, paying appropriate attention to what you were saying?

☐ ☐ If the telephone rang, was it handled appropriately? (Was it ignored or automatically forwarded? It would be inappropriate for the therapist to answer the phone during a session. This is your time.)

Yes No

☐ ☐ Did you feel you could be honest and open, or at least imagine that you could be as your relationship develops?

☐ ☐ Did you get the sense that the therapist respected and supported you?

☐ ☐ Did he provide you with adequate feedback?

☐ ☐ Did you feel you maintained enough control of the interview to feel comfortable?

☐ ☐ Did you feel you were able to discuss issues important to you?

☐ ☐ Did you feel that you "clicked" with the therapist?

☐ ☐ Did the therapist have you fill out a screen?

☐ ☐ If so, have you discussed the results?

☐ ☐ Did the therapist ask you a set of questions to determine if you are suffering from a particular type of problem, such as depression or substance abuse? In your opinion, should these types of questions have been asked?

☐ ☐ Did the therapist make a diagnosis or give you focused feedback on the issues you feel are important? Did he raise issues you had not considered but which may indeed prove critical?

☐ ☐ Do you *like* the therapist?

If you answer fourteen or more of these affirmatively, you are on your way to a good working relationship. Any less than twelve, and you should look for another therapist.

7

THE BOTTOM LINE
The Financial Aspects of Therapy

You may have decided that therapy is what you need, and even found a therapist you like. But now you are faced with a question: Can you afford it? Perhaps your insurance company refuses to cover the therapist you have chosen. Maybe your managed care company has deemed you ineligible for coverage or will only pay a minuscule amount. Paying for therapy should not add to your headaches or fears.

Managed Behavioral Care

As any newspaper reader knows, the Clinton administration's attempts to revolutionize the health care industry disintegrated in the early 1990s. What the efforts did accomplish, however, was to introduce the subject of health care at the American dinner table and political roundtable. Some of these key issues are important to grasp as you wade into the health care industry via the therapist's office.

The goal of managed behavioral care is to monitor and control the use of mental health and substance abuse services, specifically focusing on costs, while maintaining the quality of care. There are several types of managed care systems: health maintenance organizations (HMOs), preferred provider organizations (PPOs) and managed behavioral health care companies (MBCs). Each one provides numerous services, including approving initial treatment and designating the initial length of care to be granted. (This is referred to as precertification.)

Managed behavioral care was spawned by the staggering health care bills forced upon consumers and the employers. Estimates indicate that in 1992 America spent $700 billion on health care, with between $17 billion and $20 billion spent on mental health care.[1] During the late 1980s and early 1990s, when the economy was feeling the effects of international competition, American companies scrutinized their budgets and found that health care costs far outdistanced cost-of-living increases. "Manage these costs!" the bean counters cried, including costs for mental health. The companies did so, in droves. Roughly 85 percent of companies with more than one thousand employees turned their mental health coverage over to specialized managed care organizations.[2]

DR. MASI SPEAKS OUT: I found evidence of wanton extravagance during my time as director of employee counseling at the U.S. Department of Health and Human Services in the 1980s. A number of employees were involved in psychoanalysis sessions four days a week, all on the federal government tab. The employer—again, a government agency—was also charged with one hour sick leave a day for time spent at each session.

There is no doubt about it: The proliferation of managed care companies has dramatically changed the face of mental health care. Gone are the days when insurance companies blindly paid high hourly rates for treatment with questionable outcomes. Unlike HMOs, MBCs do not directly provide care. Instead, "gatekeepers" and "case managers" point clients in the direction of clinicians who have contracted with them and agreed to certain payment scenarios. The industry relies on a highly competitive selection process for clinicians, offering its clients a finite, preselected list of such practitioners from which to choose. It stresses the value of shorter treatment and often recommends second opinions in cases of questionable diagnoses. The focus is on short-term, goal-oriented mental health care. Many of the firms dictate the least expensive course of treatment, often over the objections of therapists.

This trend has dealt mental health professionals a staggering blow. In 1993, more than 60 percent of psychologists responding to a San Francisco–area study said their incomes had declined because of managed care.[3] Although many may not feel this is such a bad thing, perhaps more ominous for the consumer, nearly one-third of the respondents said that a nonclinical case manager had insisted that a client be treated with drugs despite the therapist and client's opposition. More than half of the psychologists felt that the case managers were inadequately trained, and a whopping 44 percent said they were considering leaving the field altogether because of managed care.

These trends offer both positive and negative outcomes for the consumer. They could mean that your insurance will not pay for the mental health treatment you need. On the other hand, you are much less likely to end up in unmonitored therapy that drags on indefinitely. After all, someone other than you and the therapist is considering the value and nature of your treatment.

Long-Term Versus Short-Term/Brief Therapy

Based on the goals you've defined with your therapist, you have the option of embarking on brief, short-term therapy or long-term therapy. Brief therapy will focus on a single area of concern and will be very goal specific. Brief therapy can last from one to eight sessions, is focused on one goal and is often used within an EAP framework. Short-term therapy focuses on several goals, however, with one or two usually being the most prevalent. Long-term therapy usually means a commitment of six months to two years, with one year being the most common.

Since the late 1980s, when managed care began to really take hold in the United States, the mental health field has come under careful scrutiny. Managed care companies found that in countless cases, intensive long-term psychotherapy or hospitalizations were being used when, in fact, there were other short-term and less costly options. Effective short-term successful measures include utilizing medication, outpatient programs and community mental health agencies. Support groups offered additional supplementation to these short-term alternatives.

Studies conducted have shown that most mental illnesses can be treated with short-term therapy. Cummings and Vandenbos state that the majority of clients treated in HMOs can be treated in brief therapy[4] when:

- The individual's level of functioning poses an imminent threat of danger to himself or others, or the inability to care for himself places the individual in a dangerous position.
- The individual has had failed treatment attempts in dealing with a chemical dependency problem.
- The individual needs highly specialized care due to certain long-term traumas. Severe child abuse that is impeding an individual's ability to care adequately for himself is an example.
- The individual needs continuous monitoring by a physician because of a serious or complicated medical condition.

What this means for you is that if you are considering embarking on a long-term relationship with your therapist, you need to consider your financial situation at the outset because chances are your insurance company or managed care company will not pay for the bulk of your treatment.

The more you learn about the mental health care business and the more strategically you think about your options, the better off you will be. This is particularly true if your employer has contracted with a managed care company or insurance company that has established specific guidelines for what mental health care costs they will cover. Under these conditions, you will likely be offered less of a selection among therapists and less financial reimbursement to see them.

> *LONG-TERM THERAPY SHOULD HAVE BEEN PUR-SUED: A twenty-eight-year-old woman with signs of severe depression is being considered for a promotion, and she is concerned that her increased absenteeism (stemming from her depression) will diminish her prospects. During her initial interview, she reveals that she was sexually abused by three male family members in her childhood. She discussed her self-described dysfunctional family at length. The counselor recommended that the client "increase social interaction . . . reduce absenteeism . . . and write a list of reasons why she deserves the impending promotion." This complex case involved multiple problems, and serious ones at that. Instead of attempting to resolve the issues in brief therapy, the peer panel felt the therapist should have recommended— in the first visit—that the client be treated in long-term therapy.*

Develop a Short-Term Budget

Before beginning therapy, try to decide what amount of money you think you can spend. Once you settle on a therapist and have seen her for a second visit, you should have an idea of how long the process will take. (The therapist will usually recommend a certain number of sessions per month.) Calculate your monthly outlay by multiplying the total number of estimated visits per month by the session rate, and then multiply that figure by the number of months that the therapist estimates you will need. You have your cost estimate.

There is a mental health benefit written into most coverage plans that may help pay the bill. If your insurance does not have such a benefit, there are other options available.

Self-Pay

In this scenario, you pay the therapist the full amount directly and apply no insurance benefit. Session rates generally range from $40 to $125 a session. Social workers and marriage and family counselors usually charge the least, and psychologists somewhat more. Psychiatrists and psycho-analysts charge the most. Rates vary dramatically based on where you live, with those in New York City and Southern California topping the list.

Self-Pay: Sliding Scale

In your first session, ask the therapist if he charges on a sliding scale. Many therapists will adjust their rate based on the client's income or current extenuating circumstances. You may also ask what can be done to reduce the rates. Some therapists will offer lower rates if you can come during the day, or on short notice, when they have cancellations.

Preferred Provider Organizations (PPOs) and Health Maintenance Organizations (HMOs)

Find out what mental health benefits your insurance company, HMO or PPO offers *before* committing to your therapist. (It should cover the first "interview" visits as well.) The most generous insurance benefits are usually offered by the military, other government agencies, secondary schools and universities. However, you may find yourself limited to the list of practitioners that the organization has sanctioned, particularly if you are with an HMO or PPO. If you are working from a provider list, be sure to refer back to the tools discussed in chapter 5 as you go about choosing a therapist. You may be charged a five-dollar to twenty-dollar copayment for each visit. Most insurance companies provide at least a five-hundred-dollar annual benefit (per calendar year) for mental health care.

Some insurance companies will let you use a therapist not included on their current list of preferred providers but impose a three-hundred-dollar to five-hundred-dollar annual deductible that you have to pay before the insurance payments begin. They tend to limit their contribution to 50 percent of the per-session fee.

In the classic "fee-for-service" model, insurance companies reimburse the therapist for the service she provides a client. HMOs receive a preset amount of money to provide health and mental health services to all their clients. Not surprisingly, getting treatment under an HMO can be much more challenging; the more dollars spent on patient care, the less is left for profit. EAPs are similar to the HMO model in that the employer pays an EAP company a flat amount to provide free short-term counseling. EAPs have not been as cost conscious as HMOs, however. If you are in a restricted HMO or managed care company, you may not be able to negotiate fees or select from a list of therapists. Therefore, you should consider utilizing your EAP.

Self-Pay/Insurance Combination

Because you will be paying the balance of what your insurance company does not cover, be sure to pin down detailed numbers on what to expect in charges from your therapist and contributions from your managed care firm and insurance company. Get a clear idea of what your out-of-pocket costs will be.

Employee Assistance Programs (EAPs)

Chances are you work for a company with an EAP but may not know it. (See chapter 5 for a discussion of these programs and inquire through your human resource personnel as to the level of services offered at your workplace.)

Nonprofit Agencies

Remember, nonprofit agencies and community service groups can also be excellent resources for those with limited income. (See chapter 5 for a discussion of the resources these groups can offer.)

Publicly Funded Care

You may be eligible for publicly assisted mental health care if your income is small. Both Medicare and Medicaid cover mental health treatment. If you are eligible, mental health centers that accept public funds are available in most communities.

Medical Hospitalization

If you or a family member is hospitalized, there are free social work and pastoral services available to you through the social service department of your local hospital.

Other Resources

If you feel you have exhausted all your options and have found nothing appropriate to your needs, you may have to go into debt or dip into savings to cover your therapy expenses. If this is the case, make a short-term commitment (say, three months) to therapy, and then reevaluate your financial situation after that time. (Obviously, if the therapist feels you need less time, then all the better.) The last thing you want is for the cost of therapy to complicate the problems you are struggling with already.

For Those on a Limited Budget

No matter what your financial situation, you can get therapy if you seek it out. There are many options available to you—you only need to be aware of them and learn to advocate for yourself.

With the inception of EAPs, therapy has become available to people who had never before pursued therapy or dreamed they'd be partaking of it. Because EAPs are available through the employer, employees often feel more comfortable seeking therapy. And because EAPs employ multilingual therapists, services are accessible to a wider population. They are also found in rural locations. In addition, it is found that men utilize EAP services more frequently than those of private practitioners.

When CNA Insurance Company surveyed their EAP clients for the first year of the program, they found that out of the five hundred participants, over 80 percent had never been in therapy before. EAPs have opened up the world of therapy to a diverse range of races, income levels and geographic locales. Although EAPs often utilize a short-term eight-session model, you can often be referred for long-term therapy if it is found appropriate. Therefore, if you are seeking therapy, it is a good idea to check with your employer to see if your company has an EAP. You may be surprised—over twenty thousand companies in the United States have EAP services for their employees.

If you are a family member or significant other of an employee of a company with an EAP, you may be eligible for services. You also do not have to tell your significant other you are seeking therapy through her EAP.

Even if you find your employer doesn't have EAP services and your budget is limited, there are opportunities open for you to obtain therapy.

Suggestions for Those Seeking Therapy on a Limited Budget

- Negotiate with a private therapist who has a sliding fee scale. (There are more than you think!)
- Check to see if EAP services are available to you.
- Call your local United Way for agencies in your community that may provide services.
- Call your local family services agency for mental health services in your community.
- Utilize your Medicaid or Medicare benefit to contract with a therapist.

Once you get a list of agency therapists or EAP practitioners, use the *Shrink to Fit* tools to select, interview and evaluate the therapist of your choice. No matter what your budget, you have the right to get the type of therapy you need.

Develop a Long-Term Budget

The cost of therapy can decimate a delicate financial situation. Proper budgeting and planning are harsh truths that must be dealt with before emotional recovery can begin. So make sure your plan is not only based on your mental health needs, but also your finances. By your second visit you should have a diagnosis, treatment plan and budget set up.

Be prepared to reevaluate your commitments of time and money during the process and as you progress. Consider the commitments you are willing to make to therapy based on the time the therapist estimates you need. Flexibility may be necessary. Does it make sense, for example, to go for a shorter period that you can better afford, then take a fiscal and emotional break and start again when you have saved up some reserves?

Don't shy away from discussing your financial situation with your potential therapist. In most cases, she should be willing to work within your budget *and* be able to meet your needs. If the therapist proves to be inflexible about the duration or cost of therapy, and you are uncomfortable with the financial picture, find another therapist. Some therapists have yet to catch up with the current fiscal and managed care climate.

On the other hand, if your financial situation is quite healthy, be discreet about divulging financial and insurance information. Otherwise you may find yourself with more therapy than you need.

When looking for therapy, never view yourself as a victim of this process. Learn what you need to get better, and become your own best advocate for making sure that it happens.

8

YOU ARE THE BOSS
Evaluating Your Therapist

You have been in therapy for a few months and are starting to feel better. Perhaps you have gained a deeper understanding of your behavior and maybe even have made some changes. On the other hand, you may simply feel confused or increasingly uncomfortable in each session and may be wondering why you started seeing a therapist in the first place. The good news is that you *can* measure your progress in therapy. It is not quite the same as determining if your broken leg has healed or if your digestive upset has passed, but you can determine if you are achieving your goals. In fact, it is important to periodically evaluate your progress in therapy, even if it seems to be going well.

The Authors' Mixed Experiences in Evaluating Therapy

The authors have evaluated the clinical work of hundreds of therapists through Masi Research Consultants. (See the

"About the Authors" section at the back of the book.) When reviewing cases of clients seeking therapy, we were often struck with how effective therapy can be in helping people get better. Many heartwarming and gratifying cases of troubled men, women, and children meeting and working with therapists showed evidence, sometimes after only a few sessions, of clients who were able to cope and function in ways they hadn't thought possible.

On the other hand, in addition to the many cases showing good, sound clinical practice, the number of those evaluated reflecting misdiagnosis and poor treatment sparked our interest in writing this book.

Troubling trends were evident. For example, some therapists were holding expired licenses. Others had little overall experience in key areas such as brief treatment and when medication could help a patient. Some were found lacking the ability to perceive a potentially violent situation. Regarding their clinical work, some were found failing to conduct basic clinical assessments and, as a result, were misdiagnosing depression and substance abuse. Others were neglecting to follow up with clients or failing to sound a warning bell when potential harm to another person was evident.

After evaluating hundreds of these cases, we reached the obvious conclusion: Consumers need to be informed and educated to receive the help they need and deserve from therapists. It is not only up to the therapist to help you feel better, it is up to you, as a potential client, to do your homework, define your problems as best you can, evaluate the process along the way, learn to trust, and be open and committed to the process.

By using the evaluation system outlined in this next section, you can help ensure you are getting the best therapy possible.

Evaluating Your Therapy

Very often in the beginning stages of therapy, or even after the first session, you will feel much better. You may experience enormous relief at having unloaded many of your troubles. These positive feelings may even prompt you to reconsider your need for therapy. This "honeymoon" sensation is a very common phenomenon, but unfortunately it is often temporary. Stick with therapy.

> *CHEATED ON BUT MOVING ON: Pat P. helped me through a bad period in my life when I found out my husband was having an affair with a coworker. She kept me focused and made it possible for me to make intelligent decisions about the rest of my life.*

Progress in therapy is never smooth or constant. As the sessions go by, you will not necessarily feel happy or good about yourself after each one. This is to be expected. Resist judging therapy—the therapist, your relationship with him and the type of therapy you are in—after one particularly negative or even upbeat session. Changing behavior is a subtle, slow, often excruciating process. It does not necessarily feel how you would expect it to. Give it enough time to take place, and share any feelings of discouragement with your therapist.

There are four general stages of therapy: assessment; talking, learning, and listening; changing behavior; and ending therapy.

Assessment

This phase usually lasts one to three sessions. During this period the therapist gathers information on you, your history, and both of you set goals that you can work together to achieve.

Talking, Learning, Listening

This phase can be anywhere from several sessions to years in the process. During this time you are discussing old, unproductive patterns of behavior, assimilating them with your history, and learning about new and healthier ways to relate. One of the primary purposes of therapy is not only to alleviate any painful symptoms you may be experiencing, but also to eliminate the unhappiness that lies beneath them. The reason why many of us repeat old, destructive patterns, is that we may eliminate a surface symptom, but not resolve the underlying pain. If you approach therapy with this goal in mind, you will work to truly change your life, rather than merely to address your symptoms. This is the hardest phase and the point where you need to really push yourself.

Changing Behavior

In therapy, change does not occur in a linear progression. You will feel as if you are stuck at certain times and zooming ahead at others. Your changes may not feel secure and solid. Stick with it—you are breaking years of old patterns and may even feel as if you are in an "emotional blender." By all means discuss this with your therapist and work to conclude what is real change and what isn't. Therapy is very stressful—there are many ups and downs in the process.

It is often difficult to define and articulate how therapy has helped you. You may just be thinking, *I don't know what I've learned, but I feel better.* Pat yourself on the back—this is a good sign!

Ending Therapy

If you feel ready to end therapy, either at the agreed-upon time or before, discuss this with your therapist. (See chapter 9 for more on ending therapy.)

Evaluating Your Therapist

You should be evaluating your therapist continually. Wait at least two to three visits, however, to consider or carry out the following:

Revisit Your *Shrink to Fit* Tools

Make it a practice to periodically return to the tools you have developed in this book so that you can measure your progress. Also, read your journal notes. Revisiting the reasons you had for entering therapy, selecting the therapist that you did, as well as the plan that you set for getting well, can be reassuring, informative and inspiring.

Progress Reports

It is not unreasonable to ask your therapist for periodic progress reports, written or verbal, in the areas that you have deemed problematic. Most therapists will not expect the request but should be happy to honor it. You should also feel comfortable asking for it.

Are *You* the Problem?

It would be absurd not to blame the professional if you could not see clearly after visiting an ophthalmologist or optometrist, or your exhaust pipe still rattled after you went to a mechanic. Therapy is different, however. Although you should consider potential shortcomings in the therapist, you are also obliged to take into account your level of commitment, possible resistance to change and the amount of work you are putting into the process. Emotional or behavioral change, so difficult and painful in the best of circumstances, can be particularly challenging when you are feeling down. At least initially, the unwanted emotions you were feeling before therapy—sadness, anger, etc.—are often less painful, and certainly more familiar, than the ones stirred up by change.

Indicators that *you* may be the source of the problem in therapy are:

- Frequently switching therapists (e.g., several times in one year)
- Missing appointments
- Chronically arriving late for appointments
- Never having the time to do the outside work suggested by your therapist (support groups, involving family members, writing in a journal, reading recommended books or articles)
- Inability to bring up issues that are painful or embarrassing, or that in any other way show you in a bad light

- Looking for alternatives to therapy—yoga, acupressure, Rolfing—before giving talk therapy a real chance
- Resistance to discussing topics your therapist brings up
- Ambivalence toward your therapist or the inability to articulate negative feelings about her

Before switching therapists or leaving therapy altogether, do yourself a favor and explore the possibility that you may be unconsciously subverting your progress. Honesty with yourself in this area is very important: More than saving you time or even money, it may help secure your future happiness.

Checklist for Evaluating Your Therapist

Answers to the following questions will help you evaluate your therapist.

The Logistics

Yes	Sometimes	No	
☐	☐	☐	Does your therapist keep appointments?
☐	☐	☐	Does he arrive on time?
☐	☐	☐	Does your therapist return telephone calls in a timely manner (i.e., within twelve to twenty-four hours unless it is an emergency)?
☐	☐	☐	Can you get an unscheduled appointment in a reasonable amount of time (i.e., within three to four days of your call)?

Personality

☐	☐	☐	Do you consider your therapist a competent professional?

Yes Sometimes No

☐   ☐   ☐   Do you feel your therapist is a good listener?

☐   ☐   ☐   Do you feel your therapist treats you with respect?

☐   ☐   ☐   Do you think your therapist likes you?

☐   ☐   ☐   Do you think your therapist challenges you when it is appropriate to do so?

☐   ☐   ☐   Do you think your therapist is supportive and easy to talk to?

☐   ☐   ☐   Do you trust your therapist?

☐   ☐   ☐   Does your therapist keep the focus on you, rather than talking too much about himself?

☐   ☐   ☐   Does your therapist maintain the confidentiality of his other clients? (For example, he never mentions the names of other clients with issues similar to yours.)

☐   ☐   ☐   Are you comfortable disagreeing with your therapist?

☐   ☐   ☐   Are you able to tell your therapist when you feel uncomfortable or angry?

☐   ☐   ☐   Do you feel you can tell your therapist just about anything?

☐   ☐   ☐   Is your therapist warm and caring toward you?

☐   ☐   ☐   Is your therapist willing to let you take some direction in the process? (For example, does she allow you to introduce a new subject and discuss it for the entire session?)

Yes	Sometimes	No	
☐	☐	☐	Does your therapist emphasize your strengths and successes?
☐	☐	☐	Does your therapist let you arrive at decisions on your own?
☐	☐	☐	Conversely, does your therapist offer you advice when you feel you need it?
☐	☐	☐	Are you able to tell your therapist about what you feel is inappropriate behavioral advice or input into your situation?

Ideally, you should be able to answer yes to at least seventeen of these twenty-two questions. If you answer affirmatively to fewer than seventeen questions, show the checklist results to your therapist and discuss your concerns with her. Bringing particular issues to light is very constructive for both therapist and client. If your therapist is resistant to criticism and unwilling to discuss your concerns, consider looking for a new one.

Examples of Therapy Gone Wrong

As in any profession, there are some therapists who are better than others. Therapists are human and make mistakes. They may misdiagnose, get off on the wrong tangents and even follow the wrong course of treatment. Bad therapy can and does happen in the full range of cases, from stress, grief, and substance abuse to mental illness and suicidal impulses. By taking more control of the process, you can help prevent bad therapy from happening to you!

A GRIEVING SPOUSE: My situation involved the loss of a spouse. I did not feel that the counselor was very well versed in handling the situation. What he said seemed very rehearsed and obvious. I felt marginally better after the first session, but not really after that. I should have seen someone else.

A MISSED MEDICAL AND DEPRESSIVE CASE: A distressed woman in her thirties received inappropriate treatment when she looked for assistance. She had lost sixteen pounds after being abandoned by her alcoholic boyfriend. She also had a fibroid tumor and indicators of depression. The counselor did not inquire about the status of her tumor, delve into the reason for her weight loss, conduct a depression screen or explore her risk for alcoholism.

MISSED ALCOHOL: A forty-nine-year-old woman under work pressure and struggling with medical problems discloses that she is suicidal (and has a plan for carrying this out) during her initial telephone interview. In the first visit the therapist determines that she has occupational problems and a nicotine and alcohol dependency. The therapist did not do the proper assessment, which would have been to conduct a suicide or MAST (Michigan Alcohol Study) screen. This client needed both assessment tools and help in the more serious directions of suicidal tendencies and substance abuse.

SUICIDAL: Ralph R., thirty-one and married, was constantly struggling with suicidal thoughts. His wife of several years was demanding a divorce, citing physical abuse and emotional neglect. No longer able to cope on his own, he requested immediate help via an emergency hotline through his workplace's EAP. Dr. Joel S., a psychologist in private practice, saw him once and diagnosed him with "reactive depression and a possible personality disorder." During their first and only session, Dr. S. ignored key warning signs of Ralph's suicidal condition and potential for more spousal abuse. He made no suicide assessment. Nor did he make any referrals—either to a psychiatrist for medication or to a suicide support center. And he did not follow up on the session with a telephone call to determine whether Ralph and his family were safe. Ralph, desperate, attempted suicide again and almost succeeded. He was immediately placed in an inpatient psychiatric hospital and is receiving costly long-term treatment. Now on disability, he is no longer able to work and is divorced. He and his former wife never speak.

SUICIDAL AND VIOLENT, SEEKING HELP: A male employee came in with increasing depression and confusion about his deteriorating relationships with two women. He reports choking the women at different times to the point of having to revive them. He also discloses a suicide attempt five years ago in which he took over-the-counter drugs with a large amount of alcohol. During the first session the therapist gives the client the phone numbers to a local emergency room and the outpatient department of a local hospital. He also refers the man to his HMO for "suicidal ideation with no current intent." The therapist did not conduct a psychiatric evaluation and instead allowed the man to leave the office with instructions to go to the emergency room on his own if he felt it necessary. This client should have been referred immediately to a psychiatrist or outpatient psychiatric program.

The sad thing about bad therapy is that the individual seeking help does not receive it. The confusion, pain and misery that led to therapy are not abated, and, in extreme cases, the therapy can even make matters worse. It is important to trust your instincts, check your progress and get another opinion if you feel your therapy is not meeting your needs.

Checklist for Evaluating Your Personal Progress

Answer these questions when conducting an evaluation of your progress in therapy. You may also consider asking your therapist and loved ones to answer with *their* observations about you.

Yes Sometimes No

☐ ☐ ☐ Do I like myself more?

☐ ☐ ☐ Do I enjoy my life more?

☐ ☐ ☐ Am I depressed less of the time?

☐ ☐ ☐ Am I getting along better with
_____ [*significant other*]?

☐ ☐ ☐ Am I getting along better with
_____ [*children*]?

☐ ☐ ☐ Am I getting along better with
_____ [*coworkers*]?

☐ ☐ ☐ Am I getting along better with
_____ [*other*]?

☐ ☐ ☐ Am I less angry?

☐ ☐ ☐ Am I less frightened or anxious?

☐ ☐ ☐ Am I crying less of the time?

☐ ☐ ☐ Am I able to make decisions on my own?

☐ ☐ ☐ Do I feel like I have more control over my
own life and destiny?

☐ ☐ ☐ Am I abusing (substances, money,
alcohol, food) less than I used to, or
better yet, not at all?

☐ ☐ ☐ Am I doing the outside work I agreed to
for my therapy, such as reading recommended material, writing in a journal,
attending support groups or Twelve-Step
meetings?

☐ ☐ ☐ Am I attending the number of appointments recommended by my therapist?

☐ ☐ ☐ Does my therapist think I am making
progress?

Yes	Sometimes	No	
☐	☐	☐	Am I happier than when I entered therapy?
☐	☐	☐	Am I proud of myself?

Hopefully you will see a general trend toward positive feelings about yourself and the process. If so, congratulations are in order—you're doing a great job! If, however, you are feeling more negative than when you started, talk over your concerns with your therapist. Consider getting a second opinion if you still feel negative at this point, or perhaps cutting your losses and quitting therapy altogether. Only you can determine the appropriate time to leave, get a second opinion or look for another therapist.

> *A DISSATISFIED CLIENT: Greg didn't understand that I needed "tools" (books, groups, exercises)—not just words—to work on my situation. But to me the "just do it" approach was only words. With the number of changes I needed to make to improve myself and my marriage, I needed something more substantial to work with, so I decided to switch therapists.*

Second Opinions

Even if your therapist's methods, treatment plan, or style make you uncomfortable or strike you as extreme, consider getting a second opinion before abandoning your current therapist. Think of doing this the same way that you would secure a second or even third opinion for a drastic or expensive medical procedure. Do not go to a therapist you might actually end up with for this second opinion. Instead, pick a respected, experienced professional who can be objective. You may choose not to tell your therapist you are getting this second opinion. But if you do, and your therapist objects to your seeking advice from another professional, consider finding a new therapist. It is completely appropriate to get another professional opinion.

Also consider getting a second opinion if your therapist recommends:

- Hospitalization
- A specific, structured inpatient program (e.g., substance abuse program, alternative therapy) that involves considerable time and financial commitment
- Separating yourself from particular family or friends if this doesn't feel right to you
- Long-term treatment (more than one year)
- Experimental, expensive or extreme alternative therapy (e.g., shock therapy)
- More than two sessions a week
- Anytime you feel uncomfortable with what the therapist suggests

Before meeting with the second therapist for a consultation, write a brief summary of your initial goals, progress and concerns as part of your own evaluation. Stay focused on the goal: getting an objective, outside perspective on the reasons for your therapist's recommendation or current course of treatment. Keep in mind that the meeting is not an opportunity to engage in another therapeutic relationship. You should be wary of a therapist who attempts to lure you away from your present situation. You should come out of this consultation with a clearer understanding of what you should do, not more confusion.

> *A DISCOURAGED CLIENT: At times I felt the therapist told me exactly what to do rather than offering several solutions and letting me choose the one best suited for my personality. I decided to leave therapy and would be reluctant to return.*

Switching Therapists

The decision to switch from one professional to another can be a delicate one. Certain warning signals should almost always prompt you to make a switch:

- The most obvious transgression of trust and abuse of power that merits switching therapists is a therapist's sexual advances. The situation happens more often than we would like to think. Damage to the client can be enormous. This sexual advance may be simply stated or conveyed to you through body language. Even if you are unsure and feel an uncomfortable "charge" in the air, leave. If an actual incident occurs, report it to the professional association of which the therapist is a member and perhaps consider taking legal action. (See chapter 3 for information on your rights as a patient.)
- The therapist talks about her own problems.
- The therapist identifies another client.
- The therapist discusses the problems of other clients without any thought to discretion and breaks confidentiality. The focus should be on you. More distressing,

perhaps, you can bet that other clients are hearing about you.

- The therapist denies the importance of what you feel is your primary area of need. This often occurs when a family member brings an addiction problem to a therapist who is inexperienced in this area and misinterprets the situation. You should also switch from a therapist who asks you to "just get over" a painful trauma, such as a divorce, assault or death of a loved one.

- You develop an unhealthy dependence on your therapist. The goal of therapy is to enable you to operate independently and make decisions for yourself, from the minuscule to the major. A highly dependent relationship with your therapist erodes the very foundation of independence and can be destructive.

- You feel humiliated, intimidated, unsafe or in any way fearful of the therapist. There are far too many unhealed healers in the therapy business. Do not assume that you are the only one with the problems. Trust your reactions and get out of a situation that seems harmful.

- The therapist displays other inappropriate behavior (aloofness, arrogance, boredom, impatience), or is authoritarian, abusive or relentlessly critical.

A DISSATISFIED CLIENT: I found the therapist to be unprofessional in some of her remarks. She talked about herself and her own problems when I was there to get help with my situation. She made some comments that I found to be offensive and insensitive regarding other people.

> *ANOTHER DISSATISFIED CLIENT: My therapist was judgmental and too directive. She did more harm than good. She obviously had her own agenda going.*

9

RUNNING ON EMPTY
When to Stop Therapy

At this point you have been in therapy for a while, have conducted periodic evaluations and life seems to be running reasonably smoothly. You have met several, if not all, of your goals and are considering leaving therapy. Some questions, fears and apprehensions may still be with you. This is completely normal and to be expected. There are, however, some unhealthy reasons for leaving therapy. How can you determine if you are really ready to be on your own?

We all know people who stay in therapy for years on end, spending countless dollars and hours while making no important decisions or progress, at least none that are evident to an outsider. How can you tell if *your* therapy has been going on too long?

The First Phase: Early Stirrings

The first impulse to stop therapy will likely bring up feelings of anxiety, and possibly a fear that you will lose any valuable ground that you gained during therapy. You may start thinking about leaving long before actually taking steps to do so. Wavering about this decision is completely normal. You may have become attached to your therapist as an "anchor" and feel that life cannot go as smoothly without him.

Keep in mind, however, that while gaining insight into your situation is important, it represents only part of a larger process. The final goal is for you to put what you have discovered into practice so that you can live an independent, productive and fulfilling life *on your own*. Wanting someone else to manage or control our lives—or confirm our every move—means that we are not autonomous.

Because the very goal of therapy is just this—autonomy, taking control of one's life—many therapists will not bring up the subject of terminating therapy until you show that you are ready to do so. Deciding that it is time to end therapy, and carrying out the task, is often proof that therapy has succeeded. In other words, thinking about leaving therapy can be a healthy sign. Even if you determine you are not ready to do so at this stage, thinking about leaving is usually an excellent first step toward autonomy. People who cannot imagine life without their therapist have not made sufficient progress in therapy.

Unless you are in a therapy situation in which the sessions are prepaid and the last session already determined, it is up to you to bring up the subject. Some unethical therapists will continue on with the process as long as you come and pay for each session—even if you had originally agreed on a smaller number of sessions. As in all facets of this process, it is up to you to make the decision to move on.

The Second Phase: Mulling It Over

Once you have gotten beyond your initial reservations and fears about ending therapy—but before actually doing it—take a look back over your journals, treatment plan, goals you defined along the way and progress reports. Take stock of your progress by revisiting why you entered therapy in the first place. Perhaps you have reached a point at which you are ready for a break or are primed to leave the process for good. As always, writing down your thoughts about this can help enormously. Discuss your thoughts about ending therapy with trusted family and friends, and see what their reaction is. Ask if they have observed positive changes. If they have, and you sense them as well, you are probably right to terminate therapy. You may be much healthier than you think!

Taking the time at this point to clearly define and evaluate your reasons for wanting to leave therapy is important for the weeks, months or even years down the road. When a crisis occurs or general malaise sets in, you may wonder why you ever walked out the therapist's door. The most likely reason for leaving therapy is your belief that you are able to cope with your problems, not that all of your problems have disappeared. You may also be ready to leave if you find yourself relatively free of tension, anger, depression and fear *most of the time*. If your personal and work relationships are satisfactory and rewarding *most of the time*, chances are you will be able to handle conflicts as they arise.

The Third Phase: Making the Decision

This is not an easy step. Most likely you have never fired anybody in your life, and you are about to tell the person who may know you better than anyone in the world that you no longer need her services. What if your wishes are not met with a positive response? Suppose the therapist thinks this is a terrible idea and tries to persuade you to stay? Should you remain in therapy under these conditions?

A therapist may question your decision to leave for several reasons:

- The therapist contends that there are deeper psychological reasons you are trying to avoid addressing by leaving therapy altogether.
- The therapist is getting "too close," and you are shrinking away in fear.
- The therapist still wants your business for selfish financial or emotional motives.
- Your therapist is having trouble letting go, meaning that it is up to you to cut the cord.

Begin to discuss your desire to leave before actually terminating. Do not walk into the office and declare it is to be the last session. Conversely, unlike an employee, you do not owe the therapist a thirty-day grace period. Ideally, the decision will be reached mutually as you discuss your reasons for leaving and the goals that you have met. Even if you do not take the therapist's advice, you should ask for and carefully listen to his thoughts on this subject.

Suppose you have tried to come to a collaborative decision, but your therapist does not share your inclination to end therapy—yet you are determined to leave. How do you deal with the guilt you may feel, considering what this person has done to help you? It is important to remember here, again, that your relationship is not a friendship. You have *paid* the therapist to *work for* you. As confusing and emotionally difficult as it might be, keep in mind that *you* are the best person to make the decision about if and when to leave therapy, regardless of what *anybody* tells you.

Checklist for Leaving Therapy

There are also good reasons for ending therapy. Work through the following checklist to help determine if you are ready to make an exit.

Yes	Sometimes	No	
☐	☐	☐	Is your need to go to therapy lessening with each session?
☐	☐	☐	Do you feel you have less and less to say? Do you find yourself rehashing previous issues and repeating old stories?
☐	☐	☐	Do you find yourself increasingly bored in your sessions?
☐	☐	☐	Is your sense of urgency to speak with your therapist about your life decreasing as you become more confident about being able to handle things on your own?
☐	☐	☐	Can you imagine life without therapy?

Yes	Sometimes	No	
☐	☐	☐	Have family members or friends noticed a positive difference in your attitude and behavior?
☐	☐	☐	Do you feel increasingly hopeful and optimistic about your future?
☐	☐	☐	Are you satisfied with the quality of the relationships with those closest to you?
☐	☐	☐	Do you have an addiction to something (alcohol, drugs) that you have successfully abstained from for longer than one year?
☐	☐	☐	Have you successfully managed several crises or bad times without resorting to old patterns of destructive behavior?
☐	☐	☐	Are you confident that you can successfully manage your life by yourself?

If you have answered affirmatively to eight or nine of the above items, you are most likely prepared to leave therapy. But before making a final decision, also review the next list. You want to be sure that you are ending therapy for the right reasons.

Unhealthy Reasons for Wanting to Leave Therapy

- You have just made a major life change that you may want to avoid discussing with your therapist.
- Your therapist has angered or disappointed you. (Try discussing this with the therapist before you decide to leave therapy.)

- You intensely dislike your therapist. (In this case, consider switching rather than leaving therapy altogether.)
- You are discouraged and frustrated by your therapist's high fees. (This has nothing to do with your progress and should be worked out in other ways.)
- You are obsessed with the idea that your therapist wants you to stay. (Rather than a lack of progress on your part, this could indicate paranoia or a reaction to your therapist's personality.)
- You have been in therapy for less than one month although you had originally contracted for a longer period.
- You have decided that change within yourself is impossible.

The Fourth Phase: Making the Move

You should spend your time in the last session going over your initial goals when entering therapy, other goals made along the way and the progress you have made. Your therapist should offer some type of summary of your therapy experience. Because you want to exit with as much confidence as possible, she should also evaluate your coping mechanisms. To do this, she may create some imaginary situations that test your feelings and reactions. How do you respond?

The last session is also a time to discuss reconnecting at some point if you feel it would be helpful. Get a clear picture of your future relationship. Do not hesitate to ask for a telephone consultation or even an actual visit during the first few months after setting out on your own. Ultimately, you should not leave this session feeling cut off or alone. It is also appropriate to check in periodically so that you can discuss your progress.

Take time in the final session, if you have not already, to let the therapist know about behavior, advice or direction that you felt was inappropriate during your time together. Ideally, the therapist will be open to hearing this kind of information and find it valuable. More important, however, it offers you an opportunity to clear your mind of any distasteful or bothersome feelings about the experience, liberating you to fully grow from the positive aspects of therapy. Sharing your thoughts on how the therapist helped you make progress can also be very helpful for his other clients.

Therapeutic Vacations

The decision to end therapy is not irrevocable. Most people do not need continuous therapy. As with your physical health, you can go years without needing psychological help. But when malaise sets in or a crisis occurs, therapy is at your disposal. Keep this in mind as you step out the door: It revolves. You can go back in if you need to. Many people use therapy in cycles, initiating the relationship to deal with a few challenging issues, taking a break and returning to deal with other issues (or altered versions of the earlier ones).

Taking a vacation from therapy is an excellent way to put into practice much of what you have been discussing and working toward. It is a way to see how well you do on your own, making your own decisions without professional help. You may fail miserably, but more often than not, you will do much better than you ever thought possible. Even if you do fail, your therapist is only a phone call away.

Can Your Therapist Be Your Friend?

There are several debates about the issue of therapists of past clients becoming friends or even forming intimate relationships. It is usually not recommended. However, just know that it can be an option to discuss if you feel it is important.

When Your Therapist Leaves *You*

Your therapist should not terminate your relationship without notice and preparation. However, the lives of therapists change, just like the rest of ours do. Yours may move, take another job, decide to stop practicing for personal reasons or die. While this can be a difficult and jolting experience, your distress can be minimized if the situation is handled properly.

> *A CLIENT LEFT BEHIND: I went to my regular session one day and was told it was the last. The therapist had suddenly decided to move. The resulting anger and distress that I felt could easily have been avoided if I had been told in advance and been properly prepared. An extra visit, phone sessions or at least a recommendation for another therapist would have made a big difference.*

A responsible therapist will give you adequate warning—several weeks—that she is planning to stop treating you. Together, you should draw up a plan for continuing on with another therapist or stopping therapy yourself. Ideally, the therapist will have names of colleagues for you to contact and should be willing to make personal introductions to break the ice. In the best of circumstances, she will be able to save you valuable time by briefing the new therapist on your situation. Try, if possible, to have several sessions with the new therapist overlap with the last few sessions with your present therapist. This should make the transition smoother.

In addition, a therapist may terminate his relationship with you if he doesn't feel progress is being made. Clients have to be moving forward in order to warrant further therapy. This may or may not be through any fault of yours. He may feel his approach is not the one to work best for you. It is important that this be discussed ahead of time and the appropriate next step—switching to another therapist, or terminating altogether—be mutually decided by the two of you.

In the case of a therapist's death his colleagues will provide referral information and, ideally, a personal introduction to other prospective counselors.

The Posttherapy Glow

Interestingly, the period *after* therapy ends may be the most productive in terms of growth and development. As you conclude this emotional journey, it may take a while for life to settle down, but you may be surprised at how well you are able to cope. Catherine Johnson, a psychotherapist and author of *When to Say Goodbye to Your Therapist*, notes that "a cognitive process goes on during this posttherapy period in which all the theories, ideas and feelings that came up in the middle of therapy get sorted out and crystallized. . . . The major lessons you've learned start to emerge."[1]

If you have gone through this process from beginning to end and have ended on a positive note, congratulations are in order! It is not easy to enter, remain in, progress through and leave therapy with a truly positive experience. *You* have a great deal to do with its success.

10

WHEN THERAPY IS NOT ENOUGH
Hospitalization and Medication

Sometimes, even with the best of attempts, therapy is not enough. You may still feel too anxious, too depressed or even suicidal. Perhaps your therapist has recommended you enter a hospital or treatment facility, or take medication. A chilling popular image comes to mind: lonely, drugged-out souls getting shoddy care—or even being ignored—in institutions where they have been placed against their will and stay for years on end. This image has been largely shaped by the media. In reality, inpatient hospitalization and medication can prove to be constructive paths toward positive mental well-being.

Inpatient Mental Health Care

When is hospitalization necessary? Simply put, when you are in danger of hurting yourself or others. Suicidal tendencies, severe depression and dissociative disorders are just a few examples of the types of problems that can require hospitalization. In some cases, you may even be hospitalized against your will as long as the proper authorities have approved of it and have determined you may be harmful to yourself or to others. Each state differs on who has the right to commit someone to inpatient hospitalization.

Inpatient psychiatric hospitals usually offer a safe place to get intensive treatment with an around-the-clock medical staff. You or the person responsible for your care should investigate the types of psychiatric programs available to you, the qualifications of the staff and the opinion of other psychiatrists or mental health professionals. Most inpatient stays are actually brief (one to two weeks long), and many patients can go on for intensive treatment in a day program, returning home in the evenings.

Day Hospital Mental Health Care

There are also psychiatric day programs available for a person suffering from mental illness. These treatment programs are run during the day, and the client goes home in the evening.

Day Hospital and Inpatient Care for the Substance Abuser

Individuals with alcohol and drug abuse or dependency problems also have several treatment options.

The Client New to Treatment

Outpatient treatment programs are typically designed for individuals who have not previously been treated for a chemical dependency. You can, in most cases, keep working during the day and go to the treatment center on evenings or weekends. Many of these programs are attached to inpatient facilities and draw on much of the same staff. Not surprisingly, the outpatient programs are less costly and involve fewer hours—from nine to twenty hours a week, depending on the client's need for structure. This kind of an outpatient program is often the first type of treatment recommended.

The Client Treated Before

The scenario is much different if you have already gone through an outpatient program or have a severe addiction that requires hospitalization and detoxification. In such cases, inpatient treatment may be necessary. Another form of treatment is a hospital day program: You stop working, spend all day there, then go home to sleep. Generally, you will be recommended for inpatient treatment if you need to be monitored, detoxified and physically evaluated. The treatment typically lasts four to seven days. If you need more care after that, you may be referred to a residential treatment center. The type of place you are referred to will partly reflect your past experiences with outpatient treatment (were they failures or successes?), the type of living situation you have (is it drug- and alcohol-free?), and whether or not you have a drug and alcohol support system. A support system usually requires regular attendance and participation in a Twelve-Step program and regular meetings with a sponsor.

In America today you have a wide variety of options to select from as you try to face up to, educate yourself about and work through an addiction. These include group support meetings, family education and treatment programs, individual therapy sessions, and classes—either voluntary or taken as part of a state-mandated program for people who have been arrested for driving while intoxicated. Inpatient treatment facilities for substance abusers vary widely in cost. Some treatment facilities look like resorts and can charge extremely high fees. Others are less lavish and can be just as effective without all the trimmings. If you are using your insurance benefit, this may determine where your treatment is provided, and the duration and kind of treatment you receive.

Halfway Houses or Residential Treatment Programs

A treatment facility or your therapist may recommend a halfway house to help you manage your addiction or mental illness. In terms of intensity of care, these lie between full inpatient and outpatient care. You live on the premises with other addicted individuals or mentally ill individuals, but go to your job every day. During the evenings, you are expected to attend group meetings and sessions. A treatment facility will usually be the one to make the referral to a halfway house if they deem it necessary after an inpatient or outpatient treatment experience.

Checklist Before Entering a Hospital or Treatment Facility

Wherever you decide to go, you, a significant other or a family member should pose the following questions to a prospective hospital or treatment facility before selecting it and checking in.

☐ Do you have a special program for my particular problem or preference (mental illness, addiction, eating disorder, women's program)?

_____

_____

☐ Is your emphasis on drug therapy, psychotherapy or both?

_____

_____

☐ Can my present therapist treat me in the hospital?

_____

_____

☐ How is your program structured?

_____

_____

☐ What is the schedule, and what will my day look like?

_____

_____

☐ How often do I meet with an individual therapist? And in a group?

_____

_____

☐ How will my release be determined? By me? My therapist? The hospital?

_____

_____

☐ What will *all* the service fees be? (Get this figure in writing.)

_____

_____

☐ What other expenses will I have to pay (prescriptions, meals, special services)?

_____

_____

☐ Is there a family component to the therapy?

_____

_____

☐ What type of program will be available to me after I am discharged?

_____

_____

☐ What if I have a relapse? Is there a treatment component built into the program, or do I have to start over?

_____

_____

Medications

As managed care spreads into all aspects of health, increasing numbers of mental health disorders are being treated with drug therapy. There are both good and bad aspects to this trend. Given the effectiveness of many of these medications, more people are able to function well and experience happiness than ever before. Many people who previously needed inpatient care can now independently hold a steady job and maintain homes and families of their own.

> *ON THE WAY TO FEELING BETTER: I had panic attacks and agoraphobia. I was quickly helped and also was referred to a doctor for medication. I am now on medication and am 90 percent better. I was desperate when I went into therapy, and I feel so much better now. I am very pleased with the therapy I received. Without Gwen K. I don't know what would have happened to me. I tried for a long time to handle it myself, but I just kept getting worse. I thank God that I used this program.*

In a common scenario, the medication relieves many of the symptoms of mental illness while psychotherapy both encourages behavioral change and deepens the individual's ability to cope with and understand her illness. This has been found to be the most effective method—utilizing talk therapy to discuss your emotional issues and taking medication to relieve the symptoms. Assuming you are not using an M.D. for therapy, you will be referred to either a psychiatrist or your own doctor for the selection of the prescription and the overseeing of the medication. If you are on medication, you should have your condition and medication dosage regularly evaluated. You should also meet with the prescribing physician to discuss side effects or any unwanted or bothersome reactions.

There are five primary categories of psychiatric medications: antidepressants; antimanics (mood stabilizers);

benzodiazepines (antianxiety agents or minor tranquilizers); major tranquilizers; and anticholinergics or anti-Parkinsonian agents.

The most common antidepressants include fluoxetine (Prozac), sertraline (Zoloft) and phenelzine (Nardil). The most common antimanic drugs include lithium (Lithobid, Eskalith), carbamazepine (Tegretol) and valproic acid (Depakote). The most common benzodiazepines include diazepam (Valium), chlordiazepoxide (Librium) and alprazolam (Xanax). The most common major tranquilizers include chlorpromazine (Thorazine), perphenazine (Trilafon) and molindone (Moban). The most common anticholinergic drugs include benztropine (Cogentin) and diphenhydramine (Benadryl).

All of these medications pose the risk of side effects. Common ones (to many, but not all, patients) include constipation, anxiety, change in sex drive, dizziness, sleepiness, weight gain, headaches, nausea, increased urination, rapid heart rate, confusion and difficulty in coordinating movements. Investigate the potential side effects of the drug you are going to start taking, and tell the physician or psychiatrist about any that develop. The physician or psychiatrist should also give you a sense of when you are likely to start feeling the medicine's effects.

Beware of a psychiatrist who tries to convince you to only see *her* for medications and therapy. You should have the option to receive medication and get *brief* medication evaluations from a psychiatrist while continuing to regularly see the therapist of your choice for counseling.

RESISTING MEDICATION: I feel the EAP services are somewhat helpful for providing a place for me to talk about my problems; however, I do not feel that my objectives were met. It was suggested that I go to see a psychiatrist for medication to treat depression. While I may be showing signs of depression, which should be expected after going through the shock of being a worker who has to move or lose my job, I don't feel that I need medication to feel good. I do not like the sensation of being forced into taking medications. I plan to deal with this on my own now.

THANKFULLY MEDICATED: Jonathan J. was exceptionally helpful. He addressed my problem, and in the same hour contacted my physician and made arrangements to start me on medication, which I did that day. He also did some research to find a psychiatrist within my neighborhood, should I need one in the future. I can't thank him enough for his help and effectiveness.

Medicating the Young

All too often, children are medicated unnecessarily as a result of a misdiagnosis. Overall, medications for depression and anxiety in children are less effective than they are in adults. A multipronged approach that includes therapy, behavior modification and parental involvement should be considered before giving a child an antidepressant. If at all possible, get a second opinion before administering a psychiatric drug to your child.

Questions to Ask Before Receiving Medication

- What is the medication?

  _____

  _____

- What are the side effects?

  _____

  _____

- How often is it taken?

  _____

  _____

- What benefit can I expect?

  _____

  _____

- How long will these benefits last?

  _____

  _____

- What happens with prolonged usage (more than six to twelve months)?

  _____

  _____

- How long will I be on it?

  _____

  _____

- How often will I be monitored?

  _____

  _____

- Who will be administering the medication?

  _____

  _____

- How often will the therapist and psychiatrist be speaking about my progress?

  _____

  _____

11

HELPING OTHERS HELP THEMSELVES
Your Loved Ones in Therapy

Your spouse is depressed, your teenage son is acting up and coming home drunk on weekends or your mother refuses to get out of bed in the morning. What can you—and should you—do when loved ones are in trouble?

As trite as it may sound, keep in mind that you cannot help those who will not help themselves. Having said that, there are steps that you can take to encourage a loved one to find help. They may not be as obvious as you think. Even if you are working out of the most altruistic of motives, you may make the situation worse by giving the person advice, trying to control her in some way or constantly pointing out where her life has taken a wrong turn. The loved one you aim to help may well grow defiant, defensive and resistant to change. It is important to remember your role is to guide a loved one to professional help, not label her or provide that help yourself.

When Your Spouse or Partner Is in Trouble

How can you tell if your spouse or partner is in trouble? This is a very tricky area. Start out by examining *yourself*. Often we blame somebody else for problems *we* are having. If you really want to help a loved one, *you* should go over the warning signs checklist in chapter 2 and take a good look in the mirror. There is the classic term *enabler,* which refers to a loved one who is enabling the troubled individual to continue the destructive behavior in which he is engaged. If you are obsessed with trying to change or control another's behavior, you may be causing a great deal of the problems you are blaming on someone else. Consider getting the opinion of a trusted friend or relative as to where the problems seem to lie. Take care to talk to the right person, however. We often end up seeking out those who will only reinforce what we believe.

> *A THANKFUL SURVIVOR: Amy helped me immensely. I came to her at a time when there was no peace in any part of my life. My son was a serious drug addict, I was in jeopardy of losing my job and my marriage had disintegrated. Amy has helped me gain back my self-esteem, not be paralyzed by the thought of layoffs, wean myself from my codependent relationship with my son and open my eyes to a very emotionally abusive marriage that I decided was best to end. I literally owe her my life!*

The role of spouse and partner in helping a loved one in need is both delicate and quite obvious in certain ways. The gap between sound communication and unhealthy criticism can prove disarmingly subtle and subjective. Avoid criticizing how the person is conducting his life; this will only create hostility and likely fail to encourage positive change.

Providing support and, perhaps, resources are the key contributions you can make. If you decide to suggest therapy, introduce the idea at a time when your communication is good and your partner may be open to hearing the suggestion. If you get a positive response, you may want to research therapists on your insurance plan and present various options. This may provide a crucial "nudge" that ensures that she will actually get help. More often than not, however, she will not be open to the idea at the first attempt. Again, it may be helpful for you to get a therapist to help *you* navigate this terrain and, perhaps, make direct recommendations.

Once in therapy, your spouse or partner may go through uncomfortable, disturbing times. He may even take out these feelings on you. Open communication, Twelve-Step programs and, possibly, a therapist of your own can prove invaluable in such cases. If your loved one is dealing with depression or other forms of mental illness, there are support groups available for you as well.

If your loved one is still resistant to therapy, there are some things you can do. The first is to go to a therapist yourself to discuss your fears and problems. There may be issues that come out that you may not have been aware of, ways you are contributing to the problem or unexpected issues of your own that may surface. Once you spend several sessions alone with your therapist, invite your spouse to come along. This has been an effective and nonthreatening way for a spouse to enter therapy. The focus is initially on you, then the both of you. Oftentimes, your spouse will seek out your therapist or one of his own. It is an honest approach, one that is not manipulative and can help a loved one in need.

If your spouse or partner refuses to see a therapist with you, then you have a different set of problems. Perhaps through your own therapy you will determine ways you can manage the situation without your spouse or partner getting help, or perhaps you will decide to leave. As you begin to take better care of yourself, you will assist your loved one whether she gets herself into treatment or not. If the situation seems to get worse, you may have some decisions ahead of you. Determine, with your therapist, if your spouse or partner's behavior is potentially dangerous, and take the appropriate steps to leave with preparation. This may involve notifying the police, locating a shelter or securing the assistance of a trusted friend. Even if you do not end up leaving, by shifting what *you* are doing in the relationship, you can have a significant impact on your loved one, who may well feel the effects of the change and, ideally, make some changes of her own.

Parents in Need

What options do you have if your parent seems to be in emotional trouble? Aging poses numerous and often overwhelming challenges, all of which the baby boom generation will increasingly have to contend with as it ages. Alcohol abuse, for example, has proved to be a growing problem, possibly due in part to the amount of time that older people spend alone. This is particularly true for elderly women since they frequently live longer than their spouses. Excellent eldercare referral services can be found in all states and provide services ranging from counseling to help in getting information on retirement housing options and health care consultations.

> *AN ELDERLY CLIENT: Dr. Steve S. helped me imple-ment the changes I needed in my life. He was benefi-cial in turning my life around from being secluded and lonely to a very active and interactive life. I now have many things going on and like to attend senior citizens' group functions. Dr. S. picked up a broken man and helped him find direction. He was very pro-fessional, and I am greatly appreciative.*

Children in Need

Letting go of a relationship with a spouse or partner is one thing, but what can you do if your child seems to be in trouble? Again, take a good look at yourself first. Are the right motives prompting you to consider therapy for your child? The first step is to determine if you think your child needs therapy because his behavior is destructive to himself (he suffers from an addiction, bed-wetting, eating disorder, depression) or to others (she is stealing, showing fierce aggression, setting fires). Or is it because he is not living up to *your* expectations in terms of grades, athletic skill, cul-tural achievement or social standing?

> *A CONCERNED PARENT: Brenda, the therapist who met with my children and me, was extremely helpful. Since I knew Brenda before (my husband and I used her during marriage counseling), we were able to promptly address our issues specific to our children. Brenda is kind, courteous and professional.*

A Therapist for Your Child or Teenager

Estimates indicate that 12 percent—or 7.5 million—of America's 63 million youngsters under age eighteen have mental, behavioral or developmental disorders. But only a fifth of those in need receive treatment. Unfortunately, recent surveys show that drug abuse continues to be on the increase—illicit drug use among eighth graders has more than doubled in the last six years.[1]

> *A TEENAGER'S CONCERNED PARENTS: My wife and I used therapy for our teenage son. What came out was interesting: Apparently we were having difficulty allowing him to grow up. The sessions helped our son to see our reasons for feeling this way, and enabled us to find ways to allow him more freedom and independence.*

Finding a good child therapist is not unlike finding a good adult one for yourself. (Teenagers should see child therapists with a specialty in their age group. They are included under the reference "child" from here on in the book unless otherwise noted.) You may, however, want to put more emphasis on finding a warm, open and caring therapist than you might for yourself. Key qualities include gentleness, caring, patience, the ability to communicate and interact on a child's level, and the capacity to treat her with respect. The therapist needs to be able to earn your child's trust and draw her out—no small challenge with a potentially frightened, shy, hostile or otherwise resistant child. This ability can only be gauged by you and your child after the first one or two sessions. Be sure to ask your child for her opinion.

> *HELPED BY THE TEAM APPROACH: I liked the way Steve J. explained how we will work together as a team—Steve, my daughter, my husband, the school teacher and myself. I also liked the fact that Steve was willing to coordinate that team.*

Child (and adolescent) therapy is a specialized area of expertise. Beware of the therapist who claims that she can treat all members of the family; be sure to check her credentials and experience. A therapist you are considering for your child should have experience with children in the same age group. For example, a therapist who works successfully with young children may not be competent to work with teenagers. When interviewing prospective candidates, get detailed information on their background and experience. Ask how many children or teenagers she has treated. This hands-on experience is more important than having a particular degree. Obviously, a therapist for your child should also have a thorough knowledge of child and adolescent development.

> *A PLEASED PARENT: My son was having problems with anxiety before taking tests. It was affecting his grades in high school. The therapy was very positive. Meeting for several sessions alone with Dr. N. gave my son the confidence to not be so nervous when taking tests, especially standardized tests. He has improved wonderfully.*

Look to guidance counselors, pediatricians, family service agencies and parents who have had children in therapy for help in finding skilled and trustworthy child therapists.

Your Child or Teenager in Therapy

The therapist will likely speak to you about your home life. Because of his commitment to confidentiality, however, you should expect there will be subjects that the therapist has discussed with your child that he will not discuss with you. Do not question or challenge this. Take your cues from the therapist. This is especially important if you have a teenager.

At some point the therapist should offer to meet with your child alone, regardless of his age. While children are sometimes viewed as the source of problems in a family, some investigation often reveals that it is more of a family pattern problem, and not just the child. The child needs to feel free to express herself. Many act out their emotions rather than verbalizing them. On the other hand, since it can be difficult to be a parent of a young child receiving therapy, a one-way mirror may be offered to you to observe the process.

A FAMILY EXPOSED: Madeline brought her six-year-old son, Jeremy, to therapy. He was acting aggressively at home and in school, having frequent tantrums, and experiencing trouble sleeping. Only when the therapist met with him alone did she get an important clue to the problem. In drawing a picture of his family, Jeremy showed his father with a bottle of beer in his hand. Jeremy, the therapist quickly determined, was not the main cause of the family's problems. The family was seen together, and the primary source of the problem was dealt with.

Your level of involvement in therapy will partly depend on your child's age. The therapist will involve you in much more of the process if your child is under ten years of age. The therapist will ask about the child's behavior at home and school. With a teenager, however, your involvement will likely be much more limited. This classic period of rebellion demands trust between the therapist and client, making it inappropriate, or even damaging, for the therapist to involve you in much of the process.

> *A CHALLENGING TEENAGER: The problem with our family was my teenage daughter. She was causing problems at home and school. It affected work because of the phone calls from her school. We received a lot of help from Jeff on how to deal with her problems. She will see Jeff alone to work with her anger. Things aren't great, but we feel like we can cope now. We have gone as a family, and my daughter has seen him alone. We have recommended others to see him as well. He is great with the kids.*

Remember that your child's therapist is not *your* therapist, even if you are paying the bills. Under certain circumstances you may have to initiate therapy with a different therapist to contend with feelings and issues stirred up by your child's therapy experience. Your own therapist may help you grapple with such feelings as guilt, remorse or anger toward your child, as well as maintain appropriate limits with your child and her therapist.

The Abused Child

If you suspect that your child has just been sexually or physically abused, immediately take him to an emergency or critical care unit designed for this purpose. You should see a physician, preferably at a children's hospital, to determine possible physical injury. Then decide whether to utilize a support group or a private therapist to help your child deal with the trauma. The hours, weeks and months after such a trauma are a particularly delicate time and must be handled with the utmost care. A children's hospital may also have valuable resources for you to draw on as the healing process begins, such as support groups and individual therapists specializing in your child's age group and type of trauma.

If you suspect child abuse of your or anybody else's child, then by all means report your suspicions to the Department of Social Services (DSS) and the police. The law requires these professionals to report your suspicions to the appropriate family services agency for investigation.

When the Child or Teenager Refuses Treatment

Sometimes a child—particularly a teenager—will refuse therapy. However, after an initial period of rebellion, he can go on to become very receptive to treatment. Often it is the most troubled child, one sent to therapy at the school or court system's insistence, who benefits a great deal from therapy once he learns to trust the therapist. Apply the same attitude to your child's mental and emotional well-being that you would to an injury or other physical problem; you would not allow him to refuse treatment, would you? You should consider involving the child by offering him a decision about choosing a therapist, and when and where to have the appointments (e.g., after school, on weekends, near home or close to school). You need to be clear about the necessity for therapy and not let him manipulate you out of it. Again, perhaps a therapist for you is in order during this process.

CONCLUSION
Wrapping It Up

*Just as we all have colds and sore throats and upset
stomachs, so we also have periods of depression, times
when we blow our top and lose control. Our capacity
to function is being affected by an emotional illness.*

—DR. WALTER MENNINGER, M.D.
PSYCHIATRIST AND PRESIDENT AND CEO OF THE MENNINGER FOUNDATION,
A NATIONAL NONPROFIT PSYCHIATRIC CENTER FOR TREATMENT,
RESEARCH, PROFESSIONAL EDUCATION AND PREVENTION

According to the National Alliance for the Mentally Ill,
more than 5 million Americans suffer from an acute episode
of mental illness each year, and one in five families is affected
by a severe mental illness. Untreated emotional pain
can do as much damage as physical distress, if not more. It
can rip families apart and wreak havoc on individuals. As
we approach the new millennium, many of the previous
century's stigmas about mental illness, substance abuse and
therapy have abated. Hundreds of thousands of Americans
are openly acknowledging the need for outside help and are
seeking out mental health professionals.

> SANITY SAVED BY THERAPY: I have nothing but
> praise for Sharon F. I was literally a mess before I
> started seeing her. Sharon helped me to deal with a lot
> of guilt and fear, and to put the pieces back together
> again. At first, I thought my visits to see her were
> going to be a waste of time. I was wrong. Now I feel
> like she probably saved my sanity. She got me through
> some very tough times. I never thought about therapy
> much until I needed it. In fact, I hardly knew it
> existed. But I am very thankful that it was there when
> I needed it.

It is strongly encouraged that you consider therapy, but also that you become informed and learn to advocate for yourself when embarking on this most important of journeys. The first step may be the hardest to take, but remember, help is really just a phone call away. Be sure to use your best and most well informed judgment when making that call. With the turbulence caused by managed care, the flooded mental health professional marketplace and the dizzying array of treatment methods available, it is imperative that you, the consumer, be fully informed. This book, used well, gives you that edge.

Appendix

Therapy: Terminology, Theories, Adjuncts and Alternatives

Although it has its roots in scientific methods and analysis, the field of therapy is also an art. It is a creative as well as a cognitive process, open to interpretation and subjective in myriad ways. Familiarizing yourself with the terminology and theories of therapy will help you understand your options and give you a sense of the wisest course of action for you to pursue. Should traditional therapy not appeal to you, or if you would like adjuncts to it, alternatives can be found here as well.

The Settings

Day Hospital

The client gets treatment on a daily basis in a hospital setting for a specified number of hours—usually six to eight a day—and returns home to sleep.

Inpatient

The client stays in a facility around the clock. Facilities include hospitals where medical care is available on-site at all times, and residential settings where the client stays all the time but medical care is provided on-site only when needed.

167

Outpatient

Treatment is provided in the therapist's office, with each session usually lasting one hour.

Common Areas of Specialization

Eating Disorders

It is important to examine the type of specialized training that a therapist claiming a specialty in eating disorders has actually obtained. Ideally she should have recently completed at least 150 training hours in eating disorders, particularly anorexia nervosa and bulimia. Some outside training hours should have been taken within the past year. An eating disorders specialist should have a team of specialists she works with, possibly including a psychiatrist, nutritionist and staff at a particular hospital.

Phobias

The therapist should be adept at treating phobias through the use of medication and behavioral therapy.

Sex Therapy

The therapist should have obtained additional training in treating sexual dysfunction. Various modalities of sex therapy include dual sex therapy (involving both sexual partners in therapy), hypnotherapy that focuses on removing the anxiety-producing symptoms and initiating an attitude change, and behavioral therapy with its emphasis on changing learned behaviors that are problematic.

Substance Abuse

The clinician involved in the treatment of chemical dependency or substance abuse should have certification in chemical dependency. These certifications are obtained through the state as well as the National Association of Drug and Alcohol Addiction Counselors (NADAAC).

Modalities

Adolescent/Teen Therapy

Therapy with adolescents is also a specific area of expertise. Techniques used by the therapist will emphasize establishing a trusting relationship with the teen. Family therapy is often a conjunct therapy. The adolescent therapist will attempt to maintain the adolescent's confidentiality unless there is a life-threatening situation.

Child Therapy

Therapy for children is considered a specialized area of expertise. Carefully examine the credentials and training of a child therapist. Depending on the age of the child, the therapist will use techniques such as role-playing, drawing, games and pictures to assess and treat the child. Family therapy is frequently used in conjunction with child therapy.

Employee Assistance Programs

The employee assistance program (EAP) is not actually a therapy modality but, rather, a counseling benefit. Under such a program, an employer pays for a predetermined number of sessions with a mental health professional for the employee and, in some cases, his family. EAP counselors will assess your problem, provide brief counseling (if appropriate), and give recommendations for treatment resources and therapists. This free, voluntary and confidential benefit for employees is very valuable and a sensible place to start if you are trying to determine what type of care and therapist you might need.

Family Therapy

The family therapist focuses on the relationship among family members. It is important to question the therapist about the breadth of his experience and how his professional orientation helps to resolve family conflicts. This type of therapy is frequently used when treating children and teenagers. The focus is not necessarily on the child but, rather, on the dynamics of all the family members. Some insurance plans do not cover family therapy; be sure to check yours before proceeding.

Group Therapy

In this type of therapy, a group of individuals who share some type of common problem are guided by a trained therapist to help each other effect change. When considering entry into a group, be sure to review the credentials of the group therapist. This area of expertise requires specialized clinical training.

Hypnotherapy

A client is placed in a hypnotic state for the purpose of recalling situations and memories that are inaccessible in the waking state. The recalled memories are subsequently explored in therapy. Hypnotherapy can be a cost-effective addition to talk therapy because it quickly uncovers information that may otherwise take years to surface. On the other hand, hypnotherapy has also been linked to "false memory syndrome," a situation in which adults recollect exaggerated or imagined memories; in such a case, there can be profoundly negative consequences for all involved.

Individual Therapy

The primary treatment relationship is between the therapist and the client. The individual engages in "talk therapy" to effect change.

Marital Therapy

The goal of marital therapy is to modify the interactions of a couple and help find new behavior patterns that improve the relationship. Many insurance plans do not cover this type of therapy; be sure to check your coverage with the insurance company and the therapist before starting.

Pharmacotherapy

In pharmacotherapy, medications are typically used in conjunction with other forms of therapy. This type of therapy addresses the biological aspects of a problem. From Prozac and Zoloft for depression to Valium and Xanax for anxiety, modern medications have had a major impact on certain types of mental illness. Such medications can only be prescribed by a psychiatrist or medical doctor who has expertise in the use of such drugs.

"Talk" Therapy

(See *Psychotherapy,* later on in this appendix.)

Common Clinical Terms

Assessment

This is the initial part of the clinical session where the therapist obtains information from the client about what issues are to be addressed in therapy. The assessment is similar to the first visit to a physician, when she determines the cause of your physical problem.

Diagnosis

The diagnosis is made following the assessment. It is a classification made according to the fourth edition of the American Psychiatric Association's *Diagnostic and Statistical Manual of Mental Disorders (DSM-IV).* This classification system allows the therapist to put clinical information in a framework recognizable to all mental health professionals.

If you are not using insurance, there is an assessment model used in the field of social work called the Person in Environment (PIE), which looks at you in the context of your environment and other social factors, rather than only at the symptoms of your emotional issues, as might be done in one-on-one, insurance-reimbursed talk therapy.

Referral

There are instances when a therapist will recommend that the client pursue additional types of therapy, such as biofeedback or group therapy, or see a clinician specializing in a particular area of need. When making a referral, the client is given the contact information and, ideally, an introduction to the resource person.

Screens

These are used in the assessment process to get a more complete understanding of what is occurring with a client. A therapist may conduct a structured interview (technically, a test) with predetermined questions. These screens can be easily and quickly administered. The therapist should review his findings with you. Some frequently used screens are:

Beck Depression Inventory-II (BDI-II). This screening tool for depression consists of twenty-one groups of statements including subject areas such as sadness, guilt and suicidal thoughts.

Brief Symptom Inventory (BSI). This is a fifty-three-item self-report inventory designed to help the therapist in determining how a client is feeling at that point in time. It is not a measure of personality.

Drug Abuse Screening Test (DAST). This test aims to assess the extent of problems related to drug misuse. The final score indicates the severity of the drug abuse problem.

Michigan Alcoholism Screening Test (MAST). This widely used test assesses alcohol abuse. Some experts have challenged the reliability of the test, recommending that other interview tools be used in conjunction with it.

Treatment Plan

Once the diagnosis is determined, the therapist decides how therapy should proceed. The client is usually consulted as aspects of the treatment plan are hammered out. The focus of the work, the frequency of sessions and, in the brief therapy models, the specific goals to be reached are all parts of a standard treatment plan. (See chapter 6 for more on developing a treatment plan.)

Therapy Models

Behavior Modification

This model was developed as an alternative to the psychoanalytic approach. It takes the perspective that an individual's problems are not driven by the subconscious, but by learned responses. The therapy emphasizes changing the present behavior rather than searching for the root cause.

Brief Therapy

With the advent of managed care and the pressure to keep costs down, the popularity of brief therapy has increased. This model uses a specific number of sessions. Formerly, brief psychotherapy consisted of twenty sessions. Today's model usually includes one to three sessions. The focus is on quickly establishing an alliance between the therapist and the client, an active teaching role on the part of the therapist, the use of a contract—an agreement between the therapist and client regarding what the client agrees to do within a specified time frame—and homework assignments. A definite number of sessions and a termination date are established at the beginning. Brief therapy is not appropriate for psychotic individuals or those with chronic phobia, drug or alcohol addiction, active suicidal or homicidal tendencies, or other potentially destructive or severe behavior.

Cognitive Therapy

In this form of short-term therapy, the emphasis is on solving the problem(s) at hand. Its success relies heavily on the therapist's ability to rapidly form a trusting working relationship with the client. The focus is on the present and replacing negative thoughts or behaviors with affirming and positive ones. Contracts made between therapist and client, homework assignments, and the development of new skills are important aspects of cognitive therapy. Cognitive therapy has proved effective for treating mild to moderate depression (sometimes in conjunction with medication), panic attacks, obsessive-compulsive disorders, paranoid disorders, psychosomatic illness and eating disorders.

Empowerment Model

This is a model of therapy most often used in social work. It looks at the individual's relationship to class and gender, sometimes within a political environment. It has often been used with working-class women in cases of battered women's syndrome and in situations involving substance abuse.

Intermittent Therapy

This model is used when the client wants to focus intensely on a particular issue for two to five sessions, then come back again in several months for follow-up or to work on another issue.

Psychoanalysis

The model of psychoanalysis is a method developed by Sigmund Freud at the turn of the twentieth century. Freud's emphasis was on free association; the client is instructed to say whatever thoughts come into his mind. By doing this, unconscious thoughts and feelings rise to the level of consciousness (awareness). A large measure of attention is paid to the individual's first six years of life, which are considered key to determining the adult personality. Emphasis is placed on irrational, biological and instinctual forces. Later developments in this theory included social and cultural factors. Psychoanalysis requires a long-term commitment on the part of the client, who in a typical case will attend therapy three or more times a week. Change comes about through increased self-awareness. Psychoanalysis makes the most sense for individuals who are able to make long-term commitments of time and money in the effort to resolve long-standing inner conflicts. Most insurance plans do not cover this type of treatment.

Psychotherapy

This generic term refers to the "talk" therapies created to help an individual change his perceptions, feelings and behavior. The task is accomplished through the relationship between the client and a trained therapist who has learned specific techniques and interventions.

Rational-Emotive Therapy

This school of therapy was developed over the past thirty years. It combines thinking and feelings with deciding and doing, with a strong emphasis on present events. It stresses the notion that what we believe strongly influences our feelings and behaviors.

Reality Therapy

Developed only recently, reality therapy emphasizes the individual's responsibility in therapy. Focusing on the concepts of right and wrong behavior, it is most often utilized in groups where accepting the consequences of one's behavior is a key element. The individual's strengths are emphasized, as are ways to build on them to achieve success. Reality therapy is frequently used in treatment centers for troubled youth, by law enforcement agencies and in prisons.

Adjuncts to Therapy

While engaged in the therapy process, you may seek (or your therapist may suggest) adjuncts such as support groups or Twelve-Step programs.

> *HELPED WITH ADJUNCTS TO THERAPY: Dr. D. enabled me to gather up strength to get through the difficulty of facing my mother's death. I particularly appreciated his positive approach to solving problems, his referrals for other forms of self-help (i.e., support groups), and practical solutions and suggestions such as reading material.*

Support Groups

Most communities offer a variety of support groups. Some have a professional mental health counselor act as a leader and charge a fee. Examples of support groups that do not necessarily have a professional leader include Parents and Friends of Lesbians and Gays (P-FLAG) and Codependents Anonymous (CODA), a program for people with codependencies. Two additional examples of support groups for substance abuse are Self-Management and Recovery Training (SMART) and Women for Sobriety. Rational Recovery, based on the principles of rational-emotive therapy, does not have a spiritual component, nor does it rely on a Twelve-Step structure. There are also support groups for caregivers; single parents; individuals with cancer, AIDS and other chronic or terminal illnesses; and those who are experiencing grief from the loss of a loved one. Look in your telephone book or contact your local family services agency for listings.

Twelve-Step Programs

These programs are most helpful as adjuncts for individuals with addiction problems and the families (or other loved ones) who are struggling to have a good relationship with these individuals. These programs are free to attend, have no designated leader and allow you to remain anonymous. They also do not require that you participate. Brochures available at the meetings help guide newcomers. Obtaining a sponsor to help guide an individual is an important part of the program. A sponsor is a person who has achieved several years of sobriety or recovery within a specific program. She acts as a support and can help an individual better understand the program. Meetings typically take place at many different times throughout the day, at numerous locations, and late into the evening and on holidays. Consult your local phone book for the group nearest you.

The most widely known Twelve-Step program, and the basis for most others, is Alcoholics Anonymous. Support groups that share the same principles and concepts include

Al-Anon and Ala-Teen, both for family members. Narcotics Anonymous is for drug abusers, and NARACOM is for their families. Other Twelve-Step programs include Debtors Anonymous, Overeaters Anonymous, Gamblers Anonymous, Adult Children of Alcoholics (ACOA) and Sexual Addicts Anonymous.

Alternative Therapies

Deciding whether to use another type of therapy to supplement or to substitute for standard therapy can be challenging. The advantage to many of these alternatives is that they are often free or cost the individual much less than most standard therapies. Unfortunately, many people waste time and money on these methods without ever really getting to the root of their problems. If you decide to try one of these approaches, understand that they do not deal directly with the emotional aspects of a problem. Working with the tools in this book and your therapist should help bring forth alternatives that will help you in your quest to feel better.

Acupressure

This type of therapy is similar to acupuncture but involves finger pressure instead of needles to balance the body's energy.

Acupuncture

This therapy has its roots in China and is used to treat physical as well as mental health problems. Needles are used to stimulate points on the channels of vital energy, or qi (pronounced "chee"), that are believed to flow through the body and influence the body's natural balance of energy and health.

Aromatherapy

Essential oils are used to treat stress, anxiety and other emotional problems. Oils may be inhaled, massaged into the skin in diluted form or placed in baths. Aromatherapy is often used in conjunction with massage therapy, acupuncture and other holistic treatments.

Biofeedback

This method is gaining popularity in treating substance abuse, childhood trauma, depression, attention deficit disorder, chronic pain and insomnia. By placing noninvasive electrodes connected to an electroencephalogram (EEG) on the scalp, brain activity is measured and training instituted for the client to learn how to produce and sustain a more relaxed brain wave pattern. The client learns how to gain control over physical reactions.

Chiropractic

The chiropractor manipulates the spine's vertebrae in the belief that misalignments caused by poor posture or trauma cause pressure on the spinal nerve roots. This misalignment is believed to lead to diminished physical and mental functioning and illness.

Exercise

Many people consider exercise an antidote to stress and mild depression due to its inducing the release of endorphins, natural chemicals in the brain that bring on feelings of well-being and euphoria.

Massage

There are many different types of massage therapy. Some of the most popular are:

Muscular therapy. This general term refers to a range of bodywork methods and practices that have therapy as a goal. It can range from less intensive Swedish massage to deeper muscle work.

Polarity therapy. This "natural" health care system is based on the belief that energy fields and currents exist everywhere in the universe, and that the correct flow and balance of this energy in the human body is the foundation of health. Bodywork, diet changes, exercise, and attitude and lifestyle alterations may be just a few of the things that the client and therapist work on together.

Reflexology. This therapy is based on the notion that specific points on the feet and hands correspond to certain organs and tissues in the body, and that applying pressure to these points will relieve a range of stress-related illnesses.

Rolfing. This approach involves the use of intensive manipulation of the connective tissue to restore the body's natural alignment. According to proponents, this alignment can become damaged through injury, emotional trauma and poor posture.

Meditation

The term *meditation* encompasses a diverse range of methods. These methods share the belief that when the student trains herself to focus her attention, the body and mind can be brought together in unity. Meditation is often recommended to relieve stress and anxiety, due to the feelings of calm that meditation can produce.

Yoga

A series of physical poses and other body-mind exercises are used to encourage mental and physical well-being. Yoga emphasizes the interrelationship of body, mind and the body's energy.

NOTES

Chapter 2

1. Sheryl Gray Stolberg, "Gray Matter: Breaks for Mental Illness: Just What the Government Ordered," *New York Times*, 4 May 1997, D1.

2. Erica Goode, "Getting Off the Couch for Good," *U.S. News and World Report*, 23 Jan. 1989, 6.

3. T. H. Holmes and R. H. Rahe, "The Social Readjustment Rating Scale," *Journal of Psychosomatic Research* 11 (1967): 218.

4. Katherine Graham, *Personal History* (New York: Alfred Knopf, 1998), 301.

5. Clea Simon, *Madhouse: Growing Up in the Shadow of Mentally Ill Siblings* (New York: Doubleday, 1997), 40.

Chapter 3

1. Sheila Macdonald, ed., "Update for Chapters on *Jaffe vs. Redmond*: Spin-Off Case That Protects EAP Records," Employee Assistance Professional Association (EAPA) *Legislative and Public Policy Newsletter* 3 (summer 1997): 7.

Chapter 4

1. Marg Mills, "United States Has 114 Behavioral Health Professionals per 100,000 Population," *Open Minds: Industry Statistics* (Sept. 1997): 12.

2. Ibid.

3. Norman Winegar, *The Clinician's Guide to Managed Behavioral Care* (New York: Haworth Press, 1996), 6.

4. Telephone conversation between Michael Lane and Robin Masi Kuettel, February 1998.

5. I. Whiting, "Memorandum: Legal Regulation of Social Workers," *National Association of Social Workers,* 28 March 1990, 1.

Chapter 7

1. Dale Masi, *Evaluating Your Employee Assistance and Managed Behavioral Care Program* (Troy, Mich.: Performance Resource Press, 1994), 64.

2. Carol Hymowitz and Ellen Joan Pollock, "Cost-Cutting Firms Monitor Couch Time As Therapists Fret," *Wall Street Journal,* 13 July 1995, A1.

3. Ibid.

4. Nicholas Cummings and G. Vandenbos, "General Practice of Psychology," *Professional Psychology: Research and Practice,* 10 (1979): 430.

Chapter 9

1. Erica Goode, "Getting Off the Couch for Good," *U.S. News & World Report,* 23 January 1989, 62.

Chapter 11

1. P. Davis and P. Thomas, "In Affluent Suburbs, Young Users and Sellers Abound," *Washington Post,* 14 December 1997, A1.

REFERENCES

Alexander, Christopher J. *Gay and Lesbian Mental Health*. New York: Haworth Press, 1998.

Barnhill, John and Nadine Taylor. *If You Think You Have an Eating Disorder*. New York: Dell Books, 1998.

Bass, Ellen and Laura Davis. *The Courage to Heal: A Guide for Women Survivors of Child Sexual Abuse*. New York: Harper & Row, 1988.

Bozarth, Alla Renée. *A Journey Through Grief: Gentle, Specific Help to Get You Through the Most Difficult Stages of Grieving*. Minneapolis: CompCare Publishers, 1990.

Brinegar, Jerry. *Breaking Free from Domestic Violence*. Center City, Minn.: Hazelden, 1992.

Butler, Katy. "The Shadow Side of Therapy: When Therapy Does Harm." *Networker* (November/December 1992): 14–29.

Carnes, Patrick. *Out of the Shadows: Understanding Sexual Addiction*. Minneapolis: CompCare Publishers, 1992.

Carter, Rosalynn. *Helping Someone with Mental Illness*. New York: Times Books, 1996.

Cummings, Nicholas and G. Vandenbos. "General Practice of Psychology." *Professional Psychology: Research and Practice*, 10 (1979): 430.

Davis, Laura. *The Courage to Heal Workbook: For Women and Men Survivors of Child Sexual Abuse.* New York: Harper & Row, 1990.

Davis, Laura and Janis Keyser. *Becoming the Parent You Want to Be.* New York: Broadway Books, 1997.

Davis, P., and P. Thomas. "In Affluent Suburbs, Young Users and Sellers Abound." *Washington Post,* 14 Deccember 1997: A1.

Delts, Bob. *Life After Loss: A Personal Guide Dealing with Death, Divorce, Job Change and Relocation.* Tucson, Ariz.: Fischer Books, 1988.

Elliott, Karen. *The Twelve Steps of Alcoholics Anonymous.* New York: Harper/Hazelden, 1974.

Evans, Patricia. *The Verbally Abusive Relationship: How to Recognize It, How to Respond.* Holbrook, Mass.: Adams Media Corporation, 1992.

Fensterheim, Herbert and Jean Baer. *How to Conquer Your Fears, Phobias and Anxieties.* Green Farms, Conn.: Wildcat Publishing, 1997.

Frances, Allen, M.D., Michael First, M.D. and Harold Pincus, M.D. *The Essential Companion to the DSM-IV Guidebook.* Washington, D.C.: American Psychiatric Press, Inc., 1995.

Glazer, William and Nancy Bell. *Mental Health Benefits: A Puchaser's Guide.* Brookfield, Wis.: International Foundation of Employee Benefit Plans, 1993.

Goode, Erica. "Getting off the Couch for Good." *U.S. News and World Report,* 23 January 1989: 6–8.

Graham, Katherine. *Personal History.* New York: Alfred Knopf, 1998.

Handly, Robert and Pauline Neff. *Anxiety & Panic Attacks: Their Cause and Cure.* New York: Fawcett Books, 1985.

Hauer, Martin. *Teen Addiction.* New York: Ballantine Books, 1995.

Holmes, T. H., and R. H. Rahe. "The Social Readjustment Rating Scale." *Journal of Psychosomatic Research* 11 (1967): 218.

Hymowitz, Carol and Ellen Joan Pollock. "Cost-Cutting Firms Monitor Couch Time As Therapists Fret." *Wall Street Journal,* 13 July 1994: A1.

Jordan, Paul and Margaret Paul. *From Conflict to Caring.* Minneapolis: CompCare Publishers, 1989.

Knapp, Caroline. *Drinking: A Love Story.* New York: Delta, 1997.

Kramer, Peter. *Listening to Prozac.* New York: Viking Press, 1993.

LeVert, Suzanne. *When Your Child Has a Chronic Illness.* New York: Dell Books, 1995.

Macdonald, Shelia, ed. "Update for Chapters on *Jaffe vs. Redmond:* Spin-Off Case That Protects EAP Records," Employee Assistance Professional Association (EAPA) *Legislative and Public Policy Newsletter* 3 (summer 1997): 7.

Masi, Dale. *Evaluating Your Employee Assistance and Managed Behavioral Care Program.* Troy, Mich.: Performance Resource Press, 1994.

Masi, Dale and Peverley Jo Reyes. *Productivity Lost: Alcohol and Drugs in the Workplace.* Arlington, Va.: LRP Publications, 1998.

Mellan, Olivia. *Overcoming Overspending.* New York: Walker & Co., 1995.

Milam, James R., and Katherine Ketcham. *Under the Influence: A Guide to the Myths and Realities of Alcoholism.* New York: Bantam, 1981.

Mills, Marg. "United States Has 114 Behavioral Health Professionals per 100,000 Population." *Open Minds: Industry Statistics* (September 1997): 12.

Molloy, William. *Caring for Your Parents in the Senior Years: A Guide for Grown-Up Children.* Buffalo, N.Y.: Firefly Books, 1996.

Pearman, Roger R., and Sarah C. Albritton. *I'm Not Crazy, I'm Just Not You: The Real Meaning of the 16 Personality Types.* Palo Alto, Calif.: Davies-Black Publishing, 1997.

Preston, John D., et al. *Consumer's Guide to Psychiatric Drugs.* Oakland, Calif.: New Harbinger Publications, 1997.

Rapoport, Judith L. *The Boy Who Couldn't Stop Washing His Hands: The Experience and Treatment of Obsessive Compulsive Disorder.* New York: Signet, 1991.

Sachs, Judith. *When Someone You Love Has AIDS.* New York: Dell Books, 1995.

Schwartz, Arthur and Ruth Schwartz. *Depression: Theories and Treatments.* New York: Columbia University Press, 1993.

Seligman, Martin. *Learned Optimism.* New York: Pocket Books, 1990.

Simon, Clea. *Madhouse: Growing Up in the Shadow of Mentally Ill Siblings.* New York: Doubleday, 1997.

Stolberg, Sheryl Gray. "Gray Matter: Breaks for Mental Illness: Just What the Government Ordered." *New York Times,* 4 May 1997: A1.

Walter, John and Jane Peller. *Becoming Solution-Focused in Brief Therapy.* New York: Brunner/Mazel, 1992.

White, Barbara J., and Edward J. Madara. *The Self-Help Sourcebook: Finding & Forming Mutual Aid Self-Help Groups.* Denville, N.J.: American Self-Help Clearinghouse, 1992.

White, Robert and Deborah Wright. *Addiction Intervention.* New York: Haworth Press, 1998.

Whiting, I. "Memorandum: Legal Regulation of Social Workers." *National Association of Social Workers,* 28 March 1990: 1.

Winegar, Norman. *The Clinician's Guide to Managed Behavioral Care.* New York: Haworth Press, 1996.

Woititz, Janet Geringer. *Adult Children of Alcoholics.* Deerfield Beach, Fla.: Health Communications, Inc., 1990.

Wood, Barbara. *Raising Healthy Children in an Alcoholic Home.* New York: Crossroad, 1992.

INDEX

ABOUT THE AUTHORS

Background

Dr. Dale Masi is a professor at the University of Maryland's School of Social Work, and is an adjunct faculty member of the College of Business and Management. She is also responsible for the dual-degree M.B.A.–M.S.W. program. She is CEO of Masi Research Consultants (Masi), a company that specializes in designing and evaluating behavioral–health-care programs. The evaluation of programs for employees with mental-health, substance-abuse and emotional problems—called employee assistance programs (EAPs)—has been her primary focus. She has also been a Fulbright scholar.

Her experience as an appointee to the Mental Health Advisory Board of IBM has added to her expertise in monitoring their entire psychiatric benefit program. In addition, for four years she evaluated clinical programs for one of the nation's largest employers, the U.S. Postal Service, an organization with more than eight hundred thousand employees and 2 million family members. For the last fifteen years she has monitored the clinical programs of a wide variety of companies and institutions, including American Management Company, Bristol-Myers, the Internal Revenue Service, Merrill Lynch, Toyota and the U.S. Senate. She has audited programs providing clinical services through some of the largest mental-health–care delivery corporations in the world, such as Human Affairs International and Merit.

Recently, she spent time in the United Kingdom and Hong Kong, helping private industry to establish clinical standards criteria for providing services. She is the author of eight other books, including *AIDS: Issues in the Workplace* and *Evaluating Behavioral Healthcare Programs.*

Robin Masi Kuettel is a writer and an artist. As editor and researcher for five of Dr. Masi's books, she has served as senior staff member for the clinical review teams for Masi. She is writing a reference book/Web project entitled *Contemporary Women Artists: A Biographical Dictionary* for Oryx Press and several screenplays, including *Vanishing Point* and *Return of the Vixens.* She has exhibited her abstract-figurative drawings and paintings throughout the United States for over fifteen years and currently teaches multimedia and the methods and techniques of fine art at the School of the Museum of Fine Arts, Boston and the University of Massachusetts at Lowell.

Masi Research Consultants

For over fourteen years, Masi Research Consultants (Masi) has been responsible for reviewing the clinical work of therapists. Along with teams of nationally recognized psychiatrists, psychologists and social workers, Masi has reviewed and rated the work of large and small programs, including those in the public and private sectors. To date, 5 million employees—approximately 12.5 million persons including family members—have been affected by the clinical reviews conducted by Masi Research Consultants.

The therapists reviewed by Masi work within EAPs and managed mental-health–care programs. It is through the clinical review process that their work has been evaluated. Masi also evaluates the credentials of therapists working in EAPs for their clients.

The important thing to note about these clinical programs is that the therapists who staff them—90 percent of whom hold master's degrees in social work or doctoral degrees in psychology—also maintain private practices. Through these clinical reviews, Masi Research Consultants has most likely evaluated a therapist similar to the one you are about to hire or may already be seeing.

Inspire the Spirit

A Dog of My Own

Ben's wish comes true when his mom finally says he can have a puppy. But, on the way to pick up the puppy, Ben and his friend Kelly stumble upon a discovery that could change everything!
Code 5556, hardcover, $14.95

The Braids Girl

When Izzy helps Grandpa Mike with his volunteer work at the Family Togetherness Home, the girl in the corner with the two long braids makes a lasting impression on her. But, Izzy just can't seem to make the braids girl happy!
Code 5548, hardcover, $14.95

Little Souls

The Goodness Gorillas
The friends of the Goodness Gorilla Club have lots of great plans! But what will they do about Todd, the meanest kid in the class?
Code 505X, hardcover, $14.95

The Best Night Out with Dad
Danny has a new friend, and an important decision to make. Will he get to see the circus after all?
Code 5084, hardcover, $14.95

The Never-Forgotten Doll
Ellie wants to give a special gift to Miss Maggie, the best babysitter in the world. But everything is going wrong! How will she show Miss Maggie how much she loves her?
Code 5076, hardcover, $14.95

Available in bookstores everywhere or call 1-800-441-5569 for Visa or MasterCard orders. Prices do not include shipping and handling. Your response code is BKS.

Books to Nurture Your Body & Soul!

Chicken Soup for the Surviving Soul

Heartwarming accounts of courageous people who found the power to battle cancer in their endless hope, unwavering faith and steadfast determination will inspire you to adopt a positive attitude, discover your faith and cherish every moment. Just what the doctor ordered for healing body, mind and soul. #4029—$12.95

Chicken Soup for the Soul® Cookbook

In the spirit of *Chicken Soup for the Soul*, these inspiring stories revisit time-honored values such as love, loyalty and courage. Each story is paired with a kitchen-tested recipe providing nourishment for both body and soul. # 3545—$16.95

Chicken Soup for the Soul® at Work

This *New York Times* business bestseller is a timely addition to the ever-popular *Chicken Soup for the Soul* collection. This volume provides a much-needed spiritual boost for readers living in an age of global markets, corporate downsizing and unstable economies. #424X—$12.95

More from the *Chicken Soup for the Soul®* Series

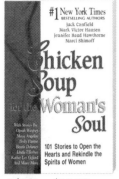
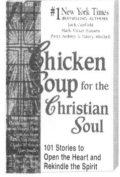

New for Kids

Chicken Soup for the Kid's Soul
Jack Canfield, Mark Victor Hansen, Patty Hansen and Irene Dunlap
Young readers will find empowerment and encouragement to love and accept themselves, believe in their dreams, find answers to their questions and discover hope for a promising future.
Code 6099, $12.95

Chicken Soup for the Teenage Soul II
Jack Canfield, Mark Victor Hansen and Kimberly Kirberger
The stories in this collection will show teens the importance of friendship, family, self-respect, dreams, and life itself.
October 1998 Release • Code 6161, $12.95

Chicken Soup for the Teenage Soul Journal
Jack Canfield, Mark Victor Hansen and Kimberly Kirberger
This personal journal offers teens the space to write their own life stories, as well as space for their friends and parents to offer them words of love and inspiration.
October 1998 Release • Code 6374, $12.95

The New Kid and the Cookie Thief
Story adaptation by Lisa McCourt
Illustrated by Mary O'Keefe Young

For a shy girl like Julie, there couldn't be anything worse than the very first day at a brand new school. What if the kids don't like her? What if no one ever talks to her at all? Julie's big sister has some advice—and a plan—that just might help. But will Julie be too scared to even give it a try?
October 1998 Release • Code 5882, hardcover, $14.95

Available in bookstores everywhere or call 1-800-441-5569 for Visa or MasterCard orders. Prices do not include shipping and handling. Your response code is **BKS**.

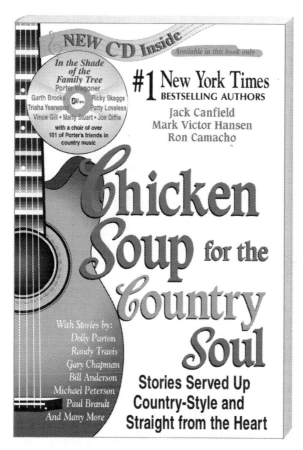

This collection captures the essence of being a woman, with true stories about love, attitude, marriage, friendship, overcoming obstacles and achieving dreams. This book will help women gain balance and a new perspective on life, and renew their faith in the human spirit.

Code 6226 • $12.95